D1474531

DETECTING AND DECIPHERING ERASED PENCIL WRITING

DETECTING AND DECIPHERING ERASED PENCIL WRITING

By

ORDWAY HILTON, M.A.

Examiner of Questioned Documents
Landrum, South Carolina

CHARLES C THOMAS • PUBLISHER
Springfield • Illinois • U.S.A.

LIGHTNING POWDER CO., INC.

1230 Hoyt St., S.E.
Salem, Oregon 97302-2121
FAX: 503-588-03-98
1-800-852-0300

© *1991 by* CHARLES C THOMAS • PUBLISHER

ISBN 0-398-05723-0

Library of Congress Catalog Card Number: 90-19416

With THOMAS BOOKS *careful attention is given to all details of manufacturing
and design. It is the Publisher's desire to present books that are satisfactory as to
their physical qualities and artistic possibilities and appropriate for their particular
use.* THOMAS BOOKS *will be true to those laws of quality that assure a good
name and good will.*

Printed in the United States of America
SC-R-3

Library of Congress Cataloging-in-Publication Data

Hilton, Ordway.
    Detecting and deciphering erased pencil writing / by Ordway
Hilton.
        p.   cm.
    Includes bibliographical references and index.
    ISBN 0-398-05723-0
    1. Writing—Identification.   2. Pencils.   I. Title.
HV8076.H55   1991
363.2′565—dc20   90-19416
                                                                            CIP

PREFACE

In this age of modern pens with self-contained ink, typewriters, word processors, and computers, what is the need of a monograph on erased pencil writing? The pencil is an old fashioned writing instrument. It dates back to the times of the quill and steel dip pens, both of which have long been obsolete. Still today it is a common writing instrument.

The pencil seldom is used to write important documents, but pencil-written documents have on occasion assumed importance after their preparation. Consider the early draft drawings of an important patent, notes written in pencil during a critical business conference at an earlier date, or the drafts of various business records which today may often be pencil written. Any of these and other pencil-written documents can be disputed and their integrity challenged.

A common challenge is to claim that the record has been altered, and if there is no obvious evidence of overwriting, it is alleged to have been erased. Pencil writing is relatively easy to erase or at least to make almost illegible. If it has been erased, what was first written? The answer may have a bearing on the importance of the erasure. In fact, document examiners with some years of practice will recognize that pencil erasures are a relatively frequent form of altered document problems.

A survey of the texts on questioned document examination and forensic science fails to show any extensive treatment of pencil erasure problems. Professional journals have published a very limited number of articles on methods of detection and decipherment. There have been those that set forth some new or modified techniques of value, but not a thorough summary of available methods for solving these problems. The purpose of the present monograph is an attempt to overcome this deficiency.

Recognizing and deciphering pencil erasures can lead to very challenging problems. There are some obvious erasures with only partial removal of the original writing. Their decipherment normally does not prove to be difficult. However, there are more thorough ones that really test the skills and perseverance of the examiner. With these problems workers should welcome an extensive source of technical information.

Assembled in this text are information on and methods for handling all types of problems relating to a suspected pencil erasure. The more important traditional methods together with some personal innovations have been used by the author. Besides these methods are a few of questionable value. The aim has been to be comprehensive in recording all suggested tests. All have been evaluated, except possibly a few more recently reported tests, such as those which require radioactive material.

What the future holds is difficult to forecast. Special equipment, such as the RCMP oblique lightbox, may be developed. Certain of these methods may suggest modifications to another examiner. The problems will continue and the methods have other applications as suggested in the final chapter. Here is a ready source of basic material set forth in the notes and references. It is hoped that this text will be of assistance to other workers in the field.

This book has gone through several revisions and reworkings over its years of intermittent preparation. In some measure each has influenced its scope and organization. While the present text is basically the author's work, he wants to acknowledge a number of worthwhile suggestions by his friend and fellow examiner, Jan Beck, of Seattle, Washington, who critically reviewed the previous draft. In addition, the comments and suggestions of his wife, Lillie A. Hilton, lead to greater clarity and improvement in writing style in the course of rewritings. He alone accepts blame for any remaining shortcomings.

CONTENTS

DETECTING AND DECIPHERING ERASED PENCIL WRITING

Chapter 1

INTRODUCTION

Pencil-written documents are very common. In all types of business and personal activities records are kept in pencil. They are usually working documents for only the occasional formal document is written with this instrument. Nevertheless, working notes and estimates, sales records, log and diary entries of various types, memoranda, and many informal writings may become important when a dispute arises about some matter to which they relate.

The vast majority of pencil-written documents are not altered in anyway. However, the reason pencil is used in preparing drafts of important papers is that changes and revisions can be easily made by simply erasing words and passages. Many other documents are kept in pencil so that corrections can be readily effected, for example, rough accounting records or the totals of more formal records of this type. Changes in pencil-written documents may be perfectly normal corrections, but on occasion an erasure can be challenged. There are instances though when the change may have been made with the intention of committing fraud. Others are made when it is believed that the original writing could be embarrassing or is not the best record or statement to have in the light of the present dispute.

Documents suspected of containing changes are often referred to a document examiner for study with the hope of disclosing evidence of fraudulent manipulation and revealing what was originally written. This group of documents represents a very small percentage of all pencil written documents. Still they become a significant number by actual count in the practice of busy examiners.

When pencil writing is submitted for examination, two questions may be raised: (1) Has there been an erasure? (2) If there was an erasure, what was originally written? These questions pertain to the technical examination, and their correct and complete solution greatly assists in reaching an accurate evaluation whether the change may have been made to deceive or with fraudulent intent. Nevertheless, even with full knowledge of what was originally written, it is not always clear if the change is fraudulent. This determination belongs to the court or jury although there are instances when the expert's findings make it relatively obvious. Every fact surrounding the preparation and subsequent history of the document may have a bearing on the determination regarding fraud. When the physical facts are properly established, they may be consistent with the claims or testimony of one party and completely inconsistent with their opponent's. Other situations may mean that the findings are only part of a series of factors that help to establish the ultimate decision. In all instances, however, the examiner's role is to retrieve as much information as possible from the document involved.

Not all pencils are alike, and some of their different qualities influence how they are erased and how the erasures are deciphered. A pencil in the minds of most people is a black lead or graphite pencil—certainly the most common kind. However, not all black pencils are the same.[1] They can be subdivided according to the qualities of the lead, especially in respect to hardness or the intensity of the stroke. In addition there are colored pencils[2] and for many years the copy or indelible pencils. Some persons use a copy pencil for more than casual documents, checks most commonly, under the mistaken notion that these pencils are "indelible" and cannot be erased.[3] Erasing of their strokes is not much different than erasing any other pencil provided the dye that is mixed with the graphite has not been moistened. It is true that when the dye has been developed by moisture, erasing becomes a more difficult but not an impossible act. While considering types of pencils one ought to include special purpose pencils such as grease pencils, china- and glass-marking pencils, and the ball pen type with liquid graphite, a writing instrument that had brief popularity in the late 1950s.[4] Every class of pencil can be erased. With each the problem of detecting and deciphering the erasure may involve different techniques and materials or special modification of standard techniques used in deciphering the common lead pencil.

The following chapters consider what is involved in erasing pencil writing and deal specifically with the various methods of deciphering the erased material. At the very outset, it should be pointed out that these problems are among the most difficult in the field of document examination and that there is no single, foolproof method to decipher every pencil erasure. It is necessary to consider and evaluate all available techniques. Despite the fact that an original paper may seem to have limited importance, due to a series of circumstances that may occur after original preparation, this previously rather unimportant pencil-written document can assume particular significance in a controversy. By the same token, with an alteration, the change itself may have far greater significance than the document in its original or altered form. The document, its erasure and the decipherment in combination can play a prominent role in controversies between parties. With the compilation of methods for decipherment and analysis of all factors relating to both erasing and deciphering of the contents, it is hoped that fewer suspected pencil erasures will remain undetected and undeciphered.

Notes

1. Zoro, J. A. and Toddy, R. N., The application of mass spectrometry to the study of pencil marks. *J Forensic Sciences, 25:* 675, 1980.
2. Hilton, Ordway, Identification and differentiation between colored pencils. *Forensic Science, 6:* 221, 1975.
3. Mitchell, C. A.: *Documents and Their Scientific Examination.* London, Griffin, 1935, chapter 6, p. 118.
4. Harrison, Wilson R.: *Suspect Documents and Their Scientific Examination.* New York, Praeger, 1959, p. 24, 100, 215.

Chapter 2

PENCIL WRITING AND HOW IT IS ERASED

PENCILS AND THEIR WRITING CHARACTERISTICS

Before one can appreciate fully what is involved in erased pencil writing problems and in the methods of decipherment or reconstruction, one should have a general understanding of the characteristics of pencil writing itself. Ordinary black pencil has a marking core containing principally a mixture of graphite and clay. In writing, flakes of graphite form the black stroke. They rub off the point and adhere to the paper surface wedged between the paper fibers. The graphite cannot and does not penetrate the paper fiber itself as ink does.

Not all pencils have the same marking qualities.[1] Some are hard, some are soft, and many fall in the midranges. In fact the number of grades of hardness and softness is extensive. Draftsmen use pencils with very hard leads, designated as 5H and 6H. At the other extreme are the very soft pencils, especially suitable for drawing and sketching. Near the center of these extremes are everyday writing pencils, but they too vary appreciably in their degree of hardness. The grade choice is in a measure a personal one. The relative hardness of the lead influences in a significant way what is encountered in both erasing the writing and deciphering what has been erased.

The hardness or softness of a pencil is controlled in the manufacturing process of the graphite core with wood pencils or the leads of mechanical pencils.[2] They are a baked mixtures of graphite, clay, a binder and waxes, and the hardness depends in part in the proportions of graphite and clay, influenced by the baking process. The details of how the manufacturer accomplishes this end result are not essential to this analysis. We need to know, however, that the differences do exist.

A pencil with a relatively soft lead requires little pressure to produce an intense, dark stroke. However, it does not hold a point long, but becomes blunt with only a small amount of writing with strokes broader and somewhat less well defined. In contrast, a very hard pencil produces a lightly-colored stroke even with heavy pressure, but it holds a sharp point for long periods of use.

The writing stroke is produced by friction of the point against the paper, friction that causes particles of graphite to rub off on the paper surface. Soft lead rubs off easily, hard, less readily. Writing pressure and the paper surface influence the friction and the intensity of the stroke. Under magnification the stroke is not a solid line but varies in intensity of color, sometimes with microscopic gaps and clumps of graphite. This pattern depends again on the hardness of the lead, the writing pressure and paper fiber pattern.

Another common part of the stroke is an embossing or groove in the paper due to the pressure on the point and its sharpness. When the writing is executed on a soft backing, such as a desk blotter or tablet, the likelihood of writing impressions is greater, and the grooves tend to be deeper than when the writing is made over a harder wood, glass, or metal surface. The intensity of pressure naturally influences the extent of embossing. Hard pencils tend to emboss more because of their sharper points and the writer's heavier writing pressure needed to compensate to some extent for the characteristic lighter deposit of graphite that is typical of a hard lead. With softer pencils, and especially with very soft drawing pencils, writing impressions are rare due to lack of need for heavy pressure and the tendency for the point to wear down quickly. It is a fact of physics, however, that with the same force on the pencil itself the sharper the point the greater the pressure per square inch on the paper with the greater likelihood of writing grooves being formed.

Not all pencil leads are the same diameter. With wood pencils this is not a highly significant factor, since sharpening creates the limited area of contact of the lead and the paper. It does, however, have some effect of the likelihood of writing grooves with the mechanical pencil. The area of contact is influenced by the lead diameter. The tip is not sharpened. Fine leads have smaller areas of contact than thicker leads, enhancing the chance of a writing groove. There is a selection of hardness with these leads as well so that it too may have some influence on whether significant writing indentations are to be found in a particular document.

The marking core of colored pencils contains various dyes or pigments, clay, a binder and wax or a wax-like substance as a lubricant.[3] In manufacturing after the lead is extruded it is hardened by drying under controlled heat for several days. The degree of hardness is controlled by the amount of binder included in the formula. These pencils mark in the same way as black pencils, leaving a colored stroke that microscopically is comparable to the graphite stroke in its varying ability to cover and in the possible presence of a writing groove. No colored pencil has the extreme hardness of the hardest black pencils. Thus extreme embossing is rare.

Wax marking pencils have a relatively hard wax-like core that is impregnated with dyes to form the thick soft marker. The points tend to be blunt so that they leave a heavy stroke virtually devoid of any embossing.

Copy pencil leads contain dyes in addition to the graphite and clay. In writing all three constituents are deposited on the paper. When the point or the written stroke is moistened the dyes develop a blue or purple color. Before moistening only a careful study under magnification enables one to distinguish between copy pencil writing and that of a comparable soft standard pencil. The former can be recognized by the grayish flakes of undeveloped dye spread along the stroke. Once the stroke is moistened and the dye developed the stroke becomes much more difficult to erase.[4] For years copy pencils had a moderate amount of use and may still be found occasionally in old pencil-written documents. Today, however, they have virtually disappeared.

One further type of pencil should be considered although it is actually a special class of ballpoint pen. It is the liquid graphite pencil.[5] Its operation and construction is exactly like the ball pen. The marking substance is a very finely ground graphite mixed with an organic vehicle. This ink is rolled on the paper by the ball revolving though the ink chamber, picking up the graphite impregnated ink and subsequently rolling it on the paper. The stroke may vary from a solid black to a black deposit on only the upper paper fibers. Under many writing conditions the ball leaves a grooved track that is continuous even when the ball pencil skips or fails to write. Heavy blots of ink and other stroke defects typical of ball pen writing may be found. With these liquid graphite pencils the bond between the graphite and the paper is stronger than in the strokes from a conventional pencil, but the writing can be erased.

The graphite pencil was introduced in the mid 1950s, saw some popularity, but finally disappeared completely during the 1960s. In 1979 an erasable ball pen was introduced.[6] Its writing can be erased with an ordinary pencil eraser when first written and for a few days afterwards. It is mentioned here only because many of the techniques for examining erased pencil writing can be applied to erasures of either of these ball pen writings.

THE ERASING PROCESS

How is pencil erased? Actually, there is only one effective method—rub the writing with a rubber eraser. In this way the graphite of black pencil writing and the colored marking of other pencils are removed. A soft art gum erases lighter pencil writing without seriously disturbing the paper fibers. When dealing with the usual pencil writing and with heavier graphite deposits art gum is very slow. Rubber erasers found on most wooden pencils and some mechanical pencils are a more effective tool. Comparable erasers are sold separately. Light rubbing with these erasers may take the pencil stroke off the paper, but usually there is some evidence of this action with disturbance of the paper fibers or a change in the paper surface finish. The existence of disturbance depends on the amount of rubbing and the quality of the paper and is most prominent with erasures on low grade, cheap paper.

A typewriter or ink eraser—a mixture of a gritty, abrasive material and rubber—works rapidly. This eraser roughens and gouges the paper very easily, but is needed to erase ballpoint pencil writing. While rapid, it does not produce as clean an erasure in many instances as the standard pencil eraser. Fiber glass erasers are available and work similarly to typewriter erasers, but are not as effective in removing pencil writing. Finally, although not commonly used, the graphite can be scraped from the paper with a knife or razor blade, but unless skillfully manipulated, the paper is seriously damaged. The writing can be erased with each implement, some more effectively than others, but seldom without leaving traces of the act.

Graphite is a form of carbon—a very inert chemical that cannot be bleached or eradicated. This means that liquid ink eradicators and bleaching reagents do not affect pencil writing. Application of hydrogen peroxide or sodium ether are said to assist in erasing pencil by breaking the bond between the pencil stroke and the paper sizing. The graphite is then removed with a soft brush or rag. Several chemical compounds are sold commercially and used by draftsmen. The material may work satisfactorly on drawing paper and tracing cloth, but it is not well suited for erasing writing from bond writing paper. Although the inability to bleach pencil writing may be generally known, occasionally a layman asks if pencil writing was erased in this way. Obviously, it could not have been.

Colored pencils and copy pencils are erased in exactly the same way as ordinary black pencil writing. Colored pencils cannot be bleached readily with commercial ink eradicators or bleaching fluid. The rubber eraser is an effective tool that when used with sufficient pressure and perseverance can remove most of the writing although critical examination of the paper normally reveals evidence of what has taken place.

Copy pencils present a special problem once the dye has been developed. Rubbing with a pencil erasure will remove all of the graphite, but the colored dye is only slightly weakened. It is necessary to then apply a bleaching solution, such as commercial ink eradicator, to remove the dye. If the liquid eradicator is applied first, it is somewhat more difficult to remove all traces of the dye, but the graphite is not affected. It must then be removed with the standard pencil eraser.

The liquid lead pencils produce strokes that resist erasing with an ordinary pencil eraser. It is necessary to use an abrasive type that is attached to the writing instrument to remove all of the graphite effectively. Afterwards one can be almost certain to find the paper surface disturbed. This difficulty in erasing may be one of the reasons that limited the popularity of this kind of pencil.

The erasable ballpoint pen has to a large measure overcome the problem of making a change in the freshly written document. Pencil erasers can remove the fresh ink and still in a reasonable length of time the ink becomes more permanent. The writer can correct his text, but the recipient should find changes more difficult.

WHAT IS LEFT?

After the pencil writing has been erased what remains, if anything? Let us assume first that all of the graphite deposit has been removed. In practice this condition is rare but with with diligent erasing can be accomplished. With no graphite remaining, a writing groove or indentation of the original writing may still remain. When an indentation does not show there may be a slight compression along the track of the writing. A more common condition is to find that not all of the graphite or the colored pencil pigment was effectively eliminated. A pencil stroke is not as easy to remove entirely as it is commonly believed. In other words there may be fragments of letters, whole letters, or fragments of words as a weak, shadowy outline left on the paper. In some instances all the original pencil writing is merely weakened, but a great deal of the original strokes remain. When the original writing was very intense, graphite is often smudged over a wide area. Method of deciphering the erased matter depends on development and interpretation of whatever remains, that is the writing grooves, the fragments of graphite or marking material, or the very weak writing itself. The ensuing chapters deal with the techniques needed to accomplish this.

Notes

1. Bradley, J. H., Sequence of pencil strokes. *J Criminal Law, Criminology and Police Science, 54:* 232, 1963.
2. Mitchell, C. A., *Documents and Their Scientific Examination.* London, Griffin, 1935, pp. 90–99.
3. Lucas, A., *Forensic Chemistry and Scientific Criminal Investigation,* 4th ed. London, Arnold, 1946, pp. 95–96. Hilton, Ordway, Identification and differentiation between colored pencils. *Forensic Science, 6:* 221, 1975.
4. See note 2 above, 118–137.
5. Hilton, Ordway, Characteristics of ball point pen and its influence on handwriting identification. *J Criminal Law, Criminology and Police Science, 47:* 612, 1957. Harrison, Wilson R., *Suspect Documents and Their Scientific Examination.* New York, Praeger 1958. pp. 24, 100, 215. Both authors report the date of introduction as early 1955.
6. Flynn, William J., Paper Mate's new erasable ink pen. *J Police Science and Administration, 7:* 346, 1979. Pfefferli, Peter and Mathyer, Jacques, "Eraser Mate" un stylo a bille a encre effacable. *Review Internationale de Criminologie et Police Technique,* 407, 1979. Hilton, Ordway, Characteristics of erasable ball point pens. *Forensic Science International, 26:* 269, 1984.

Chapter 3

HAS THERE BEEN AN ERASURE?

VISUAL EXAMINATION

Has there been an erasure? This question can be of concern to anyone who has a pencil written document before him. Often the question has been decided, not always correctly, before the document is submitted for technical examination, but on other occasions it is only suspected that something could have been erased. The correct determination may require extensive and careful examination under laboratory conditions. With an occasional document no one has suspected that a change has occurred before such an examination is made. It is a fact that not all erasures are alike. There are obvious erasures, apparent but not definite erasures, and mirage-like erasures that look as though one has been made, but the signs are misleading.

The majority of erasures are obvious. Tall letters, such as "h's" and "l's" or lower projections of "y's" or "g's," appear weak due to partial erasing along the edge of the main erasure. The area under suspicion may be badly smudged with smeared graphite. At times the rubbing may have been so extensive or the paper so poor that its surface is badly gouged or roughed (Fig. 3.1). This fact can be generally recognized by viewing the paper surface as it is held at eye level with the main source of light beyond the document. With the document held in this position the erased area may not reveal disturbed fibers but may simply reflect the light differently than the surrounding areas. This examination may also suggest or reveal that there are indentations from the previous writing. Extensive rubbing, which is normally necessary to remove heavy pencil writing or writing with a liquid graphite pencil, may actually create thin spots in the paper and in extreme instances deep gouges and actual holes and tears. The thin areas show up clearly with transmitted light when the paper is held over the light source as it is studied (Fig. 3.2). Critical examination in good light, but not bright sunlight, may disclose fragments or strokes not a part of the writing now occupying the area.

Normal viewing may reveal fragments of partially erased writing—parts of words, letters, or weak strokes (Fig. 3.3). All of these tests can be applied away from the laboratory, in an attorney's or a business office. If one or more of these warning signs are present there is good likelihood that something has been erased.

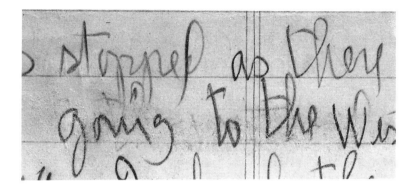

Figure 3.1. Several indicies of an erasure appear under the words "going to the We(st)." The area is slightly discolored and the paper surface has a rough appearance, the lower projection of the "p's" in "stopped" above are partially erased, there are fragmentary pencil strokes above "going" and the four words in question display a slightly darker writing than the writing above.

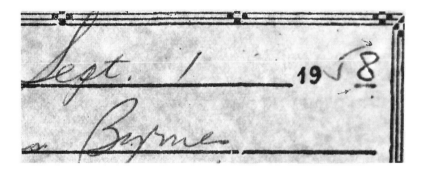

Figure 3.2. This receipt was written with a liquid pencil, and the date shows evidence of an abrasive erasure. The transmitted light photograph reveals a streak of thin paper under and above the "8." The center of the printed line beneath has been damaged by the erasing action. Thin spots may also be encountered in all types of pencil erasures.

In every case, even in the laboratory, an examination to locate an erasure should be made under different lighting conditions. Good light is essential. Subdued daylight, such as light from a north window, is

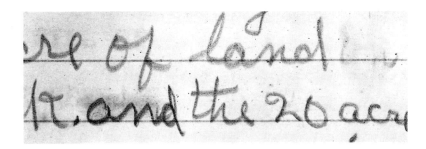

Figure 3.3. A pencil written holographic will contains several changes made by the testatrix as she wrote the document. Typical evidence of erasures appears in the partially erased "on" following the word "land" (top line), and the smudges and darker written "and" on the next line below reveals another change.

desirable. Good artificial illumination may be satisfactory. The slight red-yellow quality of tungsten lights makes it more difficult to detect weak yellow-brown stain residues of rubber erasers. However, extremely bright light is not necessarily the best illumination. Neither is fluorescent lighting from ceiling units that tend to diffuse the light throughout the room. Examinations holding the paper at eye level and sighting across the sheet reveal the most information when carried out in somewhat diffused light coming from the side. This condition can often be achieved when the viewer steps back into an area where the light strikes the paper entirely from one side and at an oblique angle. Stepping back in to a closet or an unlighted, narrow hallway is helpful. Under these conditions the rough paper surface, weak stroke fragments, or indentations and even the slightly different reflective quality of the paper surface, each a potential sign of a pencil erasure, can be discovered.

Transmitted light examination of a suspected erasure area is not universally as helpful as other types of visual study, but these should not be omitted. In the laboratory a light box or a light table is usually employed. There is some value in being able to vary the intensity of illumination although it is not absolutely essential. Diffusion of the light helps. In the field a document can be examined by holding it up to a window or in front of a light source, the former method being slightly better. Not only are thin spots and tears revealed but sometimes weak stains and smears from the erasing may be revealed.

With pencil-written documents careful microscopic or magnified study should be made of the pencil strokes. When there is evidence of a second pencil having been used, especially within a section or paragraph of the document, this area should be subjected to rigorous investigation (Fig. 3.4). Erasures are sometime made and new words inserted with a different pencil. Other times no erasure was necessary since a gap was left in the original preparation, and the second pencil becomes evidence of inserted material. In any event, however, here is a further danger signal that must be recognized and the true condition determined.

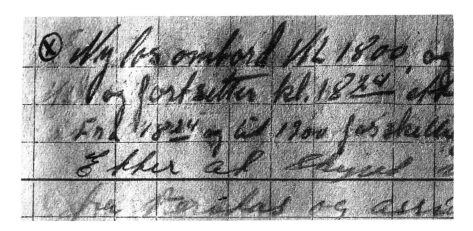

Figure 3.4. An extensive erasure was made in a ship's log book. The upper three lines were rewritten. Key evidence consists of darker writing than in the following lines together with the indentations and fragments of pencil lead that can be seen to the left of the first three lines as well as at points within the lines of writing.

The more skillfully erased writing, especially when the original writing was a light, weak stroke, may require carefully controlled examinations. For example, it may be necessary to examine the paper under very critically-directed side lighting. A microscope spot illuminator, with which the intensity of illumination can be controlled, and a low power magnifier are useful tools for revealing slight indications that the paper surface has been disturbed (Fig. 3.5). The binocular microscope may be needed, and certainly if field examinations fail to disclose concrete evidence of erasing, these tests should be made before a final decision is rendered that no erasure has occurred.

In all suspected erasures one must guard against misinterpreting the physical evidence. Some apparent erasures are only "mirage erasures." The presence of smudges, for example, may suggest that an erasure has occurred. However, they must be intelligently evaluated. The mere handling of paper, particularly with soft pencil writing, can smudge

Figure 3.5. An erasure in a motel registration card invalidated the time of registration. Note the badly disturbed area under "9:30." Low angle illumination revealed this condition and also a groove from an erased stroke through "A.M.", showing that the original registration time must have been after noon. Thus the defendant's alibi that he could not have been at the crime scene in the morning, as the prosecution witness had testified, failed. A guilty plea was entered before the resumption of the trial the following day.

writing without any erasing. Dirt, soiled fingers, or other types of smears on the paper may on first inspection look like an area of erased pencil writing, but a complete study may show that the writing was blurred by another means or the paper was only soiled, and there had been no erasure.

Writing indentation strongly suggest that pencil writing may have been erased but indentations alone are not complete proof. The question hinges on whether any fragments of graphite or other evidence of erasing can also be found. When any writing has been executed on a sheet of paper lying on the one in question, the writing indentations may simply be embossings from the second writing. No graphite would be found nor would there be evidence of rubbing with an eraser. In some instances these indentations do not accurately align with the pencil writing on the paper whereas erased indentations would. Impressed writing tends to be less sharp and intense than indentations from erased writing since the intervening paper, on which the original writing appears, weakens and broadens the resulting grooves. On the other hand, if pencil has been very thoroughly erased, microscopic graphite fragments are apt to remain (Fig. 3.6). The final decision that graphite is present normally requires study under the binocular microscope. Despite high-grade paper, extensive erasing necessary to remove all graphite disturbs or alters the paper surface and modifies its reflective quality especially when viewed at an acute angle. Indentations are found with many pencil erasures, but without other concurrent indications great care must be exercised in interpreting their cause.

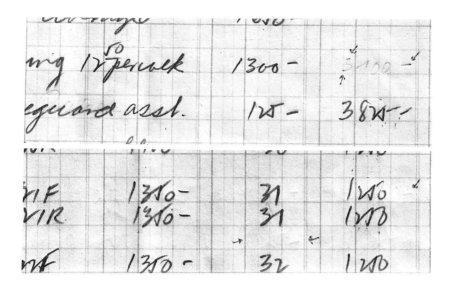

Figure 3.6. In the upper section the erasure of a subtotal is marked by arrows that contain fragments of graphite in the grooves of a "3" and a dash. The lower section contains the corresponding area of the following page. Indentations from the writing on the page above are visible and free from graphite deposits. The arrow to the right of "1250" on the upper line points to the impression from the dash after the erased "3100 -." The two arrows below "31" mark the area containing indentations from the "125 -" on the previous page. Similar weak indentations of the "25 -" can be made out. Examiners must be able to distinguish between the two classes of writing impression found in this illustration.

No examination of a document suspected of containing erasures is complete without a study of the back of the sheet. It is not infrequent that the erasing action causes smears and smudges to be picked up on the back. At times, there are small bits of writing offsets, especially when the sheet had rested on another containing soft pencil writing. Whenever deposits appear on the back of the sheet, which cannot be accounted for by any other logical explanation, the face of the sheet over this area should be very carefully studied to be sure that no erasing has taken place.

Papers with rulings, printed portions, and tinted surfaces should be studied with special emphasis on these elements. The rubbing action of the eraser can bring about a dimming of the tint around an erasure, since part of the color is actually removed. This result is particularly common with papers in which there is a light surface printing to create the color or background texture in such items as check paper. Accounting work sheets and many other commonly used papers have light ink rulings that are very susceptible to damage from even a soft rubber eraser. Black printer's ink is more resistant to pencil erasers, but while its color may not be lightened by rubbing, the surface gloss that is common to some of these inks may be dulled. Erasing of pencil on any of these papers may not show a disturbance of fibers themselves, but some other evidence may be present.

In all problems involving possible erasures it is well to make some examination under subdued lighting conditions. Weak pencil traces and other faint marks may be slightly more visible in such lighting than under more intense illumination. Its use is particularly helpful when attempting to decipher what was erased, but it should not be overlooked when seeking the suspected but barely visible erasure. There is no set rule that either bright or subdued light, low angle or near vertical illumination, or daylight or other light sources is the better illumination for locating erasures. It may be necessary to try all kinds and combination to reveal some of them.

CHEMICAL AND PHYSICAL TESTS

In the experience of this writer, chemical testing is very infrequently needed to locate the site of a pencil erasure. No reagent is available to react with the fragments of writing to reveal what was removed. The erasing process leaves some rubber deposit, or according to Harrison,[1] sulphur. There are tests available that utilize chemical reactions with these deposits and in addition there are physical tests employing finely ground powders or other materials that tend to adhere to any disturbed paper areas more readily than other parts of the document. All should be considered as a supplementary step when visual examinations do not appear to produce satisfactory results.

Chemical Tests. Undoubtedly, the oldest chemical test to reveal the site of an erasure is to fume the document with iodine. According to Mitchell[2] the method was first suggested by Bruylants[3] in 1891. The fumes are usually applied by means of a fuming tube packed with iodine crystals or the document can be hung in a fuming chest with a dish of crystals below that is heated slowly to produce the fumes. Areas erased with a rubber eraser should appear as a yellow stain while the rest of the sheet is discolored with the typical iodine stain. Early authors reported that if the erasure was made with bread crumbs the erased area would appear as a blue stain, but it is doubtful if workers today will encounter this phenomenon. Mitchell indicates a slight intensification of the writing grooves from the accumulation of iodine in them thus assisting with decipherment of the original writing. Lucas[4] points out that the iodine discoloration partly disappears in time as the document is left exposed to the air or can be removed with sodium thiosulphate. He does not believe the test is "advisable or necessary."

Dr. Wilson R. Harrison, who served in the British Home Office Forensic Laboratory System, developed and perfected several chemical or physical tests. One employs the reaction of sulphur on silver and requires no application of chemicals to the document itself.

He points out that when the paper surface is rubbed vigorously with a rubber eraser, a small amount of sulphur may be deposited.[5] The sulphur is derived from the rubber and is driven off by the slight heating created by friction between the eraser and the paper surface.

To test, a sheet of silver is polished with acetone or other organic solvent to remove the grease and oil. It is then rubbed with dilute nitric acid, washed with distilled water, and dried carefully. The metal is then placed in tight contact with the suspected paper surface for a period of several hours. The time of contact can be reduced to about one hour by the application of heat. If there has been an erasure, the area will be revealed by a brown stain on the silver. It must be noted that the test is not infallible. A blank area of the paper should be subjected to the same test, since some papers, especially tinted ones, may be contaminated by sulphur from other sources in manufacturing. A clear reaction on this latter test will confirm the accuracy of the initial one.

Physical Tests. Several tests to disclose the presence of pencil erasures depend on the altered condition of the paper, especially the disturbance of fibers and the thinning of the paper due to the abrasive action of the eraser. Dusting with powders that adhere to the loose paper fibers and the change in absorption due to actual thinning of the sheet or removal of seizing form the basis of these tests.

A recent test, developed by S. S. Kind[6] and M. D. G. Dabbs of the Home Office Central Research Establishment, England, involves the use of dyed lycode powders. The test is very simple. Stained powders are sprinkled on the sheet and the paper tapped beneath with a pencil. The powders will adhere to the area of the erasure. The adhering powder can be easily removed with paper tissues according to the authors. The test gives satisfactory results some months after erasing, and the best results are obtained with erasures made with a rubber eraser. When a plastic eraser has been used the powder adherence is weaker. It appears from subsequent tests made by the authors that the powder adheres to areas with some rubber residue present. The method of preparing the stained lycode powder is described in an earlier publication.[7]

Among other tests are three by Harrison—powdered graphite, white flourescent powder, and a weak solution of dye. In the graphite test a very fine graphite powder, such as finely divided fingerprint powder, is sprinkled on the document, the document shaken and the excess powder tipped off the paper sideways.[8] The disturbed area of the paper tends to hold the powder thus emphasising the erasure. The powder can be removed by a strong blast of air across the area. In a later publication Harrison advises against the use of this test.[9] Despite its effectiveness the graphite is very hard to remove completely. Harrison also points out the objection of courts to this test. Actually, it should be a firm rule not to apply any graphite or pencil strokes to an area suspected of being erased since fragments of graphite left after such testing may prevent others from interpreting further tests correctly because of the graphite fragments. The presence of small deposits of graphite in a suspected area can be an important clue that there has been an erasure. Therefore, any such additions to the document must be avoided.

An excellent combination for a fluorescent powder is a mixture of a fine grade talc and Lumogen UV White as the fluorescent ingredient. Harrison recommends about 20 times talc by weight to the Lumogen UV White mixed with chloroform.[10] When mixed, the wet powder is spread out, and the chloroform is allowed to evaporate without heating. Note that heat can ruin the powder. The dried mixture should then be sifted through a fine gauze. The finished powder has a strong blue-white fluorescence. Pretesting is advised because of modern fluorescent brighteners added to some papers. If there is a distinct difference in the fluorescence of the powder and the sheet, some powder should be sprinkled on the document in question and the sheet shakened. Finally, after dropping off any excess powder the document is viewed under ultraviolet light and the erased area will be revealed. Normally, the remaining powder is so limited that it will not be noticed in daylight, but, if desired, can be lifted off with a lump of Plasticine. There are other powders that can be mixed with talc to give different fluorescence if the Lumogen UV White and paper do not give contrasting fluorescence.

A nonfluorescent powder, developed at l'Institu de Police Scientifique et de Criminologie of the University of Lausanne, Switzerland, was reported by Mathyer in a privately circulated paper.[11] It is a mixture of starch and 5–10 percent methylene blue. The mixture is sprinkled on the document around the area of possible erasure and gently shaken, and the excess is tapped off of the paper. The powder adheres to the area of a rubber erasure staining it blue. This adhering powder can be removed by gentle brushing or by dabbing with Plasticine. Moore made a series of tests of the powder on different papers and found it effective with erased pencil and typewriting on writing and typewriting paper.[12] He reported that the percentage of methylene blue was not critical and was highly sensitive to the contact of rubber with the paper. Possible problems with its use are acknowledged, problems that might also be encounted with other types of powders.

A recent advance in erasure detection powders is a mixture of copy machine toner and bicarbonate of soda (baking soda).[13] The powder is handled exactly like methylene blue-starch, shaking it across the sheet where it will adhere to erased areas. When the test is completed the powder can be dusted off of the erased areas with a soft brush. Riker and Lewis had found with methylene blue-starch that even after careful dusting some microscopic particles could be found on the document. Since the methylene blue reacts with latent fingerprint developer, the fragments can be a potential problem. A search for an equally effective substitute led to this mixture of bicarbonate of soda and toner in a 5 to 1 ratio. Comparative tests were run against both methylene blue and lycole powders. Bicarbonate of soda-toner powder was equally as effective or slightly better than either of the other tested methods. Unlike lycole, which must be purchased in England, the materials for this new mixture are readily available. The toner powder does not react with any other materials including ambient humidity or fingerprint developer. Thus, the powder appears to be an improvement for detecting pencil erasures.

Since abrasive erasing needed to remove pencil writing may disturb the paper sizing or actually thin the paper slightly, Harrison suggests dipping the sheet in a dilute dye solution. More dye tends to be absorbed in the erased area, forming a revealing stain. He warns that the method is not infallible.[14] There is also the danger of permanent stain. Further, if there is any suspicion that writing impressions from the erased material might remain, the paper should not be moistened. Such action can destroy or badly weaken these impressions. Because of these potential shortcomings the test should not be used on any document having possible evidential importance.

When there is suspicion that a pencil erasure has occurred on a page of a record book or calendar pad, the following page may contain evidence of the alteration. When writing outlines are impressed on this sheet from the questioned page above after an erasure there may be evidence of additional impressions so that erased writing is intermingled with the new matter beneath the area of the suspected erasure. When the original writing was weak it may be completely removed with moderate erasing, and the paper surface may not reveal any clearcut evidence of the alteration. Subjecting this following page to examination with the ESDA may produce invisible writing pressure traces of two overlapping writings beneath the suspected area. The ESDA is a highly sensitive instrument for detecting writing pressure traces, even those that are invisible or extremely hard to read using traditional examination methods. The instrument and the problem are discussed more fully in Chapter 8.

A. Buquet has suggested the technique of betagraphy for detecting erasures.[15] The document is placed between a sheet of organic polymer stamped, "poly(methyl C-14 methacrylate)" and photographic film. After exposure the film is developed to show a dark area of the erasure. No evaluation on use of this method other than that of its author's has been reported.

SUMMARY

The problem of whether there has been an erasure in a document can normally be answered after a series of visual examinations. The observation of fragments of letters or words that have only been partially erased, the partial erasing of letters adjacent to the suspected area, disturbed paper fibers or thinning of the paper, discoloration of the suspected area typical of soiling by a rubber eraser, indentations of previous writing that align properly with the balance of the text, changes in the reflective characteristics of the paper surface, and small fragments of graphite in the suspected area are all consistent with the conclusion that pencil writing has been erased. Most of this evidence can be recorded photographically to make a record of the document's condition at the time of examination. Combination of several of these creates strong proof of an erasure.

There may be the rare instance in which the original text was written very lightly with little writing pressure and the erasing was very skillfully completed. Under these conditions visual tests may fail to reveal the erasure, but it can still be revealed by chemical tests that react to the use of a rubber eraser.

Usually chemical testing of the document generally is not needed. The results of most of the chemical tests, when effective, should be anticipated after a thorough visual examination, but they are available to use as a basic test or for further confirmation that there has been erasure. If a supplementary test is desired, dusting with lycode powder seems the best choice. Its results can be completely removed from the paper, and it can be repeated by a second examiner if needed. In combination with certain visual observations it can confirm that these apparent indications actually resulted from pencil writing having been removed by a rubber eraser.[16] Having been assured that some material has been erased we need to address the next step—to attempt to decipher what has been erased.

Notes

1. Harrison, Wilson R.: *Suspect Documents and Their Scientific Examination.* New York, Praeger, 1958. p. 108.
2. Mitchell, C. Ainsworth: *Documents and Their Scientific Examination.* London, Griffin, 1922. p. 115.
3. Bruylants: *Pharmazeut Zentralh.* 1891. p. 228.
4. Lucas, A.: *Forensic Chemistry and Scientific Criminal Investigation,* 4th ed., London, Arnold, 1946. p. 96.
5. See note 1.
6. Kind, S. S., and Dabbs, M. D. G.: The use of Lycode powders for the detection of erasures. *J Forensic Science Society, 19,* 1979, 175.
7. Kind, S. S., Watson, M., Bland, H. H. and Smith, G. B.: The individuality of tagging powders—Lycode system. *J Forensic Science Society, 18,* 1978, 165.
8. See note 1, p. 109.
9. Harrison, Wilson R.: Erasures. In Curry, A. S. (Ed.): *Method of Forensic Science,* vol. 3, New York, Interscience 1964, p. 311.
10. See note 9, pp. 311–314.
11. Mathyer, J.: A new dimension in "Questioned Document": scientific study of oil artist painting and of pencil artist drawings. A recent case. Read at the 1974 meeting, American Society of Questioned Document Examiners.
12. Moore, D. S.: Evaluation of a method using powder to detect the site of a rubber erasure. *J Forensic Sciences 26,* 1981, 724.
13. Riker, Mary A., and Lewis, George W.: Methylene blue revisited: the search for a trouble-free erasure sensitive powder. *J Forensic Sciences, 33,* 1988, 773.
14. See note 9, p. 310.

15. Buguet, Alain: New techniques for the detection of alterations in documents. *Forensic Science. 10,* 1977, 185.
16. Welch, J. R.: Lycole powders in a case of erasure. *J Forensic Science Society, 22,* 1982, 43.

Chapter 4

VISUAL METHODS OF DECIPHERMENT

GENERAL CONSIDERATIONS

Many pencil erasures can be deciphered by critical, visual examination. It is particularly true when the original writing has only been partially removed, but it can also be accomplished when slight indentations from the original writing remain in the paper, even though all the pencil graphite or color has been effectively removed. Attempts at visual decipherment are normally the first step in these problems. Oftentimes these efforts begin simultaneously with determining whether there actually has been an erasure.

The requisites for successful decipherment are good eyesight, knowledge of what to look for, examinations under appropriate lighting conditions, the use of various special examination aids, and intelligent interpretation of what is observed. Fluency in the language of the text is also desirable. Before considering the details of the various deciphering techniques, we should reconsider what may remain of the erased writing that will enable us to make a successful decipherment.

What is left after erasing depends on the intensity of the original writing, the kind of pencil used, and the skill and perserverance of the person who did the erasing. Because of these factors we may find at one extreme that no trace of the original writing remains, or at the other extreme that very little writing has been removed from the paper. The former condition can occur after a very extensive erasing of weak original writing. The latter is more common when there has been a heavy original. When the original writing was produced by a dark pencil stroke, the erasing act tends to leave prominent carbon smudges. The greatest concentration of carbon fragments may be found along the track of the original pencil stroke, but its generally smeared condition usually does not permit a very definite decipherment. In some problems microscopic study is necessary to disclose the remaining small fragments wedged into the paper fibers. These fragments alone do not necessarily assist in deciphering what was erased. Fortunately, it is rather common with erased pencil writing to find definite indentations from the original strokes. Regardless of the kind of pencil used very pronounced writing fragments may remain in certain cases, or the erasing process may only have weakened, but in no way obliterated, what was originally there. In many problems combinations of all of these conditions are present in varying degrees. Ultimate decipherment depends upon the reconstruction and interpretation of these fragments.

The kind of available light is generally a critical element in an examination. There are three significant attributes to light used to decipher erased pencil writing—its intensity, its direction relative to the paper surface, and its quality. The most desirable attributes for a particular case depend upon the nature of the writing fragments present.

Persons inexperienced in the decipherment of erasures commonly hold a misconception that the brightest light is the best to decipher an erasure. To the contrary fragments of erased pencil strokes are generally recognized more readily under moderate or low intensity illumination. In the course of any attempted visual decipherment, there is a definite advantage in being able to vary the light intensity. Slight changes in the amount of light may lead to decipherment of strokes that otherwise could not be clearly recognized.

Directional control of the light is a further decipherment aid. One of the most useful arrangements is to exclude light from all sides of the document except one. It may even be restricted so that it only strikes the paper obliquely or at a low angle to the surface. For this purpose a spotlight source serves effectively, but daylight can be utilized in this manner by simply stepping back into a narrow hallway or closet. Some examiners arrange light so that it barely grazes the surface of the sheet, but it may be desirable to vary the angle of incidence from a low of 5 or 10 degrees up to as much as 30 or 40 degrees in relationship to the paper surface. The purpose of side lighting is to emphasize any small impressions of former pencil grooves that may remain in the paper.

The direction not only should be varied in respect to the paper surface, but it should be adjusted in respect to the line of writing. The light should be directed successively from different sides of the document, from the right, from the left, from the top, from the bottom. A deep writing impression illuminated with a beam along the groove may not be as easily recognized as with the beam at right angles to the groove. The latter arrangement creates a groove shadow with highlights on its edges, thus defining it more clearly. A small tilt top stand or document holder that permits rotation of the document through 360 degrees relative to the light direction as well as tilting to change the angle of incident light relative to the paper surface is a simple, helpful device. It frees the viewer's hands and holds the document steady in an advantageous position during study.

Good illumination that strikes the paper at a more nearly vertical angle rather than obliquely may assist in studying the remaining fragments of graphite. While adjusting the lighting, high angles of incidence should not be overlooked.

There is a difference of opinion among examiners as to the best quality of light for deciphering erased pencil writing. Some prefer north daylight, that is a diffused daylight that is free from direct sunlight. Others prefer artificial light, especially a tungsten light source in a small spotlight or reflector. The color component and the degree of diffusion varies greatly between these sources. By the same token there are advantages of examining under both types of illumination and of using somewhat diffused but directionally-controlled tungsten or fluorescent light. With different problems one type may be more effective than another. The best way to be sure is to try all types on difficult erasures. Undoubtedly not all examiners would agree in these cases on a particular form of light as there is an element of personal adaptation, but at the same time the kind of paper, the characteristics of the erased pencil writing, and the extent of erasing play prominent roles in determining which is the more effective light source.

When dealing with erasures of colored pencil writing a change in color of the light source may be essential. Color filters placed between the light source and the erased area can intensify weak fragments. For example, when a red pencil entry has been erased, illumination of the area with green light can strengthen the weak red fragments making them appear nearly black against a green background, whereas light with a high red component will tend to cause the remaining writing to almost disappear.

The writer has found that visual examination on an overcast day can lead to more extensive decipherments than similar examinations made in the same way on brighter days or under artificial illumination. There is something about the quality of daylight on dull days that helps to reveal the erased writing. Possibly, the slight contrast between the erased strokes and the paper surface is enhanced, so that the fragments become more legible in the subdued light. On a bright day similar light conditions can be simulated in a measure by nearly closing venetian-type blinds.

An artificial light source permits some control of color. Colored light, such as red or green, may be of some help particularly if it contrasts with the partially erased pencil writing. On occasions selection might be made so that the light approximates the paper color. Opportunities are rare for experimenting with these techniques, but every alternative should be tried when other methods fail. Not all decipherments are achieved by standard techniques.

As previously mentioned fluorescent lighting from ceiling fixtures is not well suited for deciphering erased writing. Its diffused nature, but probably more significantly its evenness of illumination and the limited opportunity to control its direction, restricts its value. One may actually overlook an inconspicuous erasure if the document is only examined in an inside room with this type of illumination. However, a fluorescent light source is apt to work more effectively when one moves away from it so that the light strikes the document principally from one side. Diffused daylight and fluorescent lighting have a number of similar qualities. With proper control one might well be substituted for the other. The inside room, however, entirely illuminated by overhead, fluorescent units, is surely one of the poorer places to study suspected erasures.

In a few problems, examination of a suspected erasure by means of transmitted light can assist with the decipherment of the erased material. The technique is not always helpful, but this is no reason for its complete neglect. Some examiners have suggested that if the document is made somewhat more transparent by spraying with alcohol, for example, the transmitted light examination reveals greater detail. This writer has never used the technique and hesitates to recommend it. If there is any chance whatsoever that indentations from the original writing are present in the paper, wetting can weaken or remove them and may also interfere with other tests.

LABORATORY AIDS

There are a number of laboratory aids that can help in deciphering partially erased pencil writing. Except for the use of magnifiers, the others are of limited assistance and usually add little to what can be achieved by standard methods. Nevertheless, in a stubborn problem, each is a potential help, and regardless of how infrequently it may assist in the decipherment, each should be tried. It is a strange thing about pencil erasures, but regardless of how carefully any method is repeated in successive problems, the results may vary sharply.

Judicial use of magnification is common. Slight magnification, $1\frac{1}{2}$ to 3 diameters, may help; moderate, 5 to 10 diameters, helps at times and restricts at others; higher magnification has rare application. In the first place magnification tends to weaken rather than intensify the very weak strokes with which we are dealing. Furthermore, successful decipherment often results from "sudden inspiration," recognition of words and sentences from fragments of groups of words, rather than from a "letter by letter" breakthrough. Thus, when a combination of several letters and fragmentary strokes are viewed together, the examiner may begin to recognize the entire word, even though every detail of all letters is not clear. The apparent decipherment must be thoroughly tested making sure that all fragments of writing are consistent with this preliminary interpretation. Higher magnification involving study of all areas occupied by one or two key letters may need to follow. Acknowledging that this kind of solution can occur emphasizes the advantage of limited magnification in which a wide area of the erasure can be viewed as a unit. There are instances in which it can hasten the final solution. When first turning to magnification, therefore, it may be advantageous initially to limit its range between $1\frac{1}{2}$ to 3 or possibly as much as 5 diameters.

Some optical reduction helps to intensify weaker strokes, and a reducing lens has its place in solving erasure problems. Its use requires good eyesight. In general it is not the most important tool, but there are times when it can be.

Color filters have been discussed in connection with examination of erased colored pencils and as a means of altering the contrast between pencil erasures and the tinted paper background. It is well to have available thin filters that do not reduce the light intensity too much, in addition to photographic filters. Another use is to reduce the interference of stains that partially obscure erased writing fragments. Their principal, and more common use, is in photographic techniques for deciphering erasures that will be discussed in a later chapter.

The polarizing screen is a specialized light filter. It is useful in reducing glare and unwanted reflections. Some examiners have suggested examination of erased pencil writing through a Polaroid® screen, rotating it around its axis in an effort to intensify the weak writing. Techniques sometimes include illumination with polarized light. Rarely do examinations of this kind improve results. Poorer results may even be obtained on occasion. In the writer's experience it is a relatively useless method in erasure problems, Nevertheless, the technique is easy to use. In spite of indifferent results one may still wish to try it when conditions surrounding the erasure, such as one on glossy paper, suggest that polarized light should be of some assistance.

Examination under filtered ultraviolet radiation has long been recognized as an excellent means of deciphering certain classes of erased ink writing. With erased pencil writing, it has much more limited value. With fragments of color pencil writing it may be of assistance. Fragments of color pencils, especially red with bright fluorescence, may be greatly intensified under filtered ultraviolet radiation. With black pencil ultraviolet is not as effective. The combination of the absorption of partially erased graphite and the fluorescence of the surrounding paper may strengthen weak strokes a bit. The characteristic deep purple appearance of the graphite under ultraviolet radiation is also of help in establishing that apparent fragments are actually erased pencil traces and not chemical or other stains.

The infrared converter tube shows electronically the results of illuminating a document by infrared radiation. These tubes when adapted for document work may assist with visual decipherment of erased pencil writing. They may produce only slight intensification of the remaining carbon fragments. Infrared photography is much more effective.[1]

The infrared viewing device is equipped with an infrared filter, such as a Wratten 87 filter, over the lens. The suspected area of the document is illuminated with a strong tungsten light or any infrared-rich illumination. Carbon fragments absorb infrared while the paper reflects the unabsorbed light back to the viewing device. The fragments of unerased pencil will appear black against a white background. Unless graphite or other carbon and infrared absorbing material is present the method is not of assistance. It has been this writer's experience that normally when a rather successful decipherment is not achieved by other visual means before the infrared examination is made, the infrared technique is not apt to improve the results. On occasion there will be the exceptional problem in which new information is obtained. If, however, ink writing or other material covers some of the erased area and the overwriting does not absorb infrared, then the erased area will appear clear of interfering material and the pencil fragments can be studied more extensively. A particular advantage of using the infrared viewer is to learn whether the more sensitive and time consuming infrared photography should be utilized.

For some years Linton Godown has had a continuing interest in methods for contrast enhancement. He first suggested the use of a Ronchi plate as a means making writing indentations in paper more visible.[2] (A Ronchi plate is a transparent plate with finely spaced, parallel ruled lines that is primarily used for preparing halftones in photoengraving.) It can also be an aid in impressed writing problems. Since pencil erasures often contain writing indentations, the plate may also assist in deciphering erased pencil strokes.

The plate is placed with the ruling against the paper over the erased area and illuminated with a microscopic spotlight directed at the best angle to intensify the weak writing grooves. With indentations of very slight intensity, however, all traces can be lost. The writer has encountered indentations that could be partially read without the plate but with it over the document the indentations were completely invisible; with only slightly more intense indentations though they are intensified enough to make them more legible.

Normally, partially-erased writing, the grooves of which contain traces of graphite, may be more easily deciphered without a Ronchi plate rather than with it. Nevertheless, the plate is easy to use and provides another means of attempting to decipher or interpret obscure letter or words that cannot be satisfactorily read by other means.

In 1967 Godown suggested another technique for intensifying faint or partially erased writing.[3] The method employs "optical contrasters," partially transparent plates such as a "one way" mirror.[4] LOF 1071 plate is a commercial item proven useful in these problems.[5] His proposed method is to place the coated side of the plate in tight contact with the surface of the document. Since definition of the finest details depends on the closeness of contact between the reflecting surface and the face of the document a thin pad of sponge rubber or plastic beneath the document is helpful in obtaining and maintaining this intimate contact. Intense illumination is necessary from a microscope illuminator, for example, that directs the light through the glass plate and mirror coating. The best results are generally obtained in a darkened room with the light set so that specular reflections are directed away from the observer. The angle of light depends on the problem at hand. With writing indentations present low angles of illumination should be employed. The results obtained by these techniques are not spectacular, but in some instances do improve the visibility of writing traces to some extent.

A significant aid in any erasure problem is the availability of a quantity of known writing of the person who wrote the original matter. Writing is individual, and it is of significant help to know how letters of the erased writing most probably were formed. An examiner can successfully decipher an erasure without having examples of the writer's penmanship except for what is found in the unaltered parts of the material at hand, but more writing may well simplify his task and allow him to convince others that his interpretation of the decipherment is correct.

BACK OF THE SHEET

If the original writing embossed the paper, and especially if there is writing on only one side, examination of the back of the sheet often discloses as much or more than can be discovered from examination of the face. Significant disturbance of the paper fibers in the area of the erasure may cause interference in recognizing the indented strokes. In contrast the reverse side shows the embossing more clearly. It is also especially true when new matter has been written over the erasure. This overwriting may hide much of the indented fragments. If the overwriting fails to create new embossing, or if the new embossings are relatively weak, those from the original writing may be read more readily by obliquely illuminating the back side. At times these original ridges are somewhat more visible because of dirt or discoloration picked up during the erasing process. In other instances when both the overwriting and the erased writing appear interwoven on the back of the sheet, it may still be possible by careful study to read what was erased. Both oblique lighting and a mirror to view the reversed writing are helpful tools. New writing in the erased area greatly complicates the decipherment problem, but by studying both sides of the document decipherment by purely visual means is within the realm of possibility.

DECIPHERMENT PROCEDURES

The methods described in the previous sections can be applied in almost any sequence, and it is difficult to set forth any pattern of attack that is best in all cases. Often the document itself—after preliminary inspection—suggests what step to take first. Obvious evidence of writing impressions, for example, would suggest almost immediately the advantage of oblique lighting.

The writer has found that a somewhat natural approach is to first examine the document under good lighting conditions, probably employing subdued light to study the writing fragments early in the examination. Usually, this is followed by, if not worked in with, side lighting using first daylight and then, if needed, spotlights. Appropriate magnification is combined whenever desirable. When as complete a decipherment as possible has been made by these standard techniques, the various special aids that may be appropriate are employed.

It should be remembered in any attempt to decipher erased writing that adequate time is the most valuable aid. Only infrequently is a pencil erasure deciphered in a few moments, especially if more than one or two words are involved. Extensive erasures naturally require longer periods of study than one of only a single word or number.

The best results are seldom achieved when the examiner must work against time, such as examining an erasure immediately before he must testify. Occasionally, problems are presented and must be answered under these conditions, but every effort should be directed toward obtaining an opportunity to work more leisurely. Decipherments are more complete, and results may be more accurate, when a series of examinations of moderate duration are made. Three or four hours of study accumulated in two or more sessions may produce more extensive decipherments than five or six hours of almost continous study. This type of work can be extremely fatiguing so that after a relatively short time it may be that very little more can be accomplished by continuing the examination. In more than one problem going back with a fresh outlook after a rest of several hours has lead to extensive and somewhat rapid decipherment of material that at the end of the previous examination seemed almost meaningless.

In addition to the breaks in examination it should be kept in mind that it is always desirable to review the final decipherment sometime after working on other matters. The accuracy of the decipherment can then be tested more objectively, and there may well be the occasional case in which the need for some modification will be recognized.

When dealing with an erasure in which there are impressions of the original writing, there can be a slight advantage in interrupting the examination for several days. If the document is left uncovered on a desk or a file cabinet, the examiner may find the indentations somewhat more visible when coming back to the problem. This "aging process" has no scientific basis except to suggest that the writing grooves may have accumulated a slight film of dust to enhance their visibility. There may be also the effect of coming back to the problem after the interruption with a new approach that enables the examiner to see details that he had previously overlooked. This step may only be a further application of working this class of problems in easy stages for best results, but the improvements with "aging" have been observed by others than this writer.

How a decipherment is achieved varies from problem to problem. It is not unusual to begin to recognize small words soon after the study starts, especially with a partial erasure. Still parts are broken down stroke by stroke, letter by letter, until a word is reconstructed. Partial decipherment of this nature may be necessary with erased numerals. Recognition of the probable meaning of a full sentence may be achieved before all words are fully deciphered. It is absolutely necessary, however, to work on fragments of words and letters even then to be sure that the assumed meaning is correct. Final reading of an erasure may still require some filling in of blanks and the fitting of stroke fragments into the most likely incomplete words as a means of verifying them. Many complete decipherments are clearly indicated while other are completed only by interpreting the most likely meaning of words within a long text.

Notes

1. Shaneyfelt, Lyndal L.: Obliterations, alterations and related document problems. *J Forensic Sciences, 16,* 1971, 332.
2. Godown, Linton: Personal Newsletter to members of the American Society of Questioned Document Examiners, 1957, (unpublished) and personal correspondence.
3. Godown, Linton: "Optical contrasters," a new instrumental aid in deciphering faint writing and other low-contrast evidence. *J Forensic Sciences, 12,* 1967, 370.
4. Libby-Owens-Ford Co. produces several such glasses that can be obtained through wholesalers in larger cities. See note 3, p. 372.
5. LOF spec. #1071, Transparent-Mirropane-Parallel-O–Grey, chrome alloy film tinted plate glass, 45–50% reflection coated side, approximately 15% reflection, tinted side up, approximately 5% transmission. See note 3, p. 372.

Chapter 5

PHOTOGRAPHIC METHODS OF DECIPHERMENT

Although complete and accurate decipherment can be achieved by purely visual study, photography serves as a means of recording what was originally written. Photography, however, is in itself an essential tool for achieving many decipherments. It is probably the most effective tool at the document examiner's disposal. Photography accurately preserves or records the condition of the document. It helps to show that there has been an erasure and to decipher the original writing, and it can record what has been deciphered by other means. Finally, it provides the means for demonstrating to others, especially judges and jury, all of these findings.

Numerous photographic techniques are available. A few involve the use of special materials, but most do not. What is generally required is stricter control of various standard photographic steps rather than unusual techniques. A standard document photograph, that is one in which sufficient care is taken in its preparation to record maximum detail and eliminate distortion, may of itself show what the original writing was. Normally, however, there is need at least to increase the contrast slightly in the negative or final print over that of the original document. Weak fragments may be intensified sufficiently in order to permit an accurate decipherment. Judicious control of light, proper selection of emulsion, and processing procedures can lead to very satisfactory results.

Black and white photographic materials are the standard films and printing papers. Color adds little to black pencil erasures photographs and to date there has been virtually no reported use of color films as a decipherment aid.[1] There is a good selection of black and white films covering different contrast range and with established techniques for controlling or modifying these qualities in the finished negatives. Advantages of these controls will be discussed subsequently.

One important consideration in any photograph intended to decipher erased writing is the retention of maximum details. Film size is of consideration. Small films, such as 8mm or 16mm and even 35mm, require significant enlargement to produce natural size (one-to-one) prints and only with very rigid exposure and processing controls are the details retained that are possible in standard size negatives, i.e., 4 by 5 inch up to 8 by 10 or larger. Since the latter film sizes are common to well equipped document examination laboratories the methods discussed throughout the literature assumes that such film sizes are used. Photographing erased areas at natural size or slight enlargement are the common technique. However, good results should be obtained with slightly reduced negatives enlarged at least to one to one in the printing process, but natural size negatives are preferable.

Not every photographer will choose the same film, filters and developers for deciphering erased pencil writing. Familarity with specific materials is an important consideration. Equally good results may be achieved by a personal choice of these materials. Nevertheless, there are some basic methods that can be recommended, and no suggested procedure should be rejected without some careful investigation and trial.

Standard Emulsions

Good decipherments can be achieved with moderate contrast films, such as Kodak Ektapan or Commercial Ortho, or comparable fine grain films and similar products of other manufacturers (Fig. 5.1). Use of a Wratten 8 (K2) or 9 (K3) filter may improve results. Development is usually controlled by time and temperature to produce negatives of rather sharp but not extreme contrast. Again in printing, normal to slightly contrasty prints should be the goal. Higher contrast in prints that sacrifice finer details should not be blindly sought. Better results are normally acheived by introducing improved contrast in the negative rather than attempting to attain it in the printing step.

A natural size photograph usually gives the best results, although there is some advantage in enlarging on the negative to as much as 1½ or 2 diameters. A significantly greater enlargement introduces effects similar to visual examination under high magnification—spreading of the weak fragments so that they become harder to interpret and may even weaken some finer details. The degree of enlargement either in the negative or in the final print requires careful selection and possibly some experimentation with the problem at hand.

Figure 5.1. Section A is a photograph of a portion of an engineering estimate sheet. The negative was made on Panatomic-X film using normal copying procedurer[24]. A partial erasure appears after "Tower 2." In section B the decipherment has been traced over in ink. The erasure reads: "Crane and Bucket" and under "160" in the right column, "800." In section C the area was photographed with rather low angle, oblique lighting (single photoflood). In this instance some letters have been intensified because of the writing indentations. The lighting reveals the paper texture and surface irregularities causing interference with the ease of decipherment of some letters. Visual examination of the erasure had revealed writing impressions and significant pencil residue.

High Contrast Emulsions

High contrast films may improve the photographic decipherment, but are not necessarily the ultimate answer. A worker using such emulsions must become accustomed to them. In this group are such high contrast films as Kodak Contrast Process Panchromatic, Contrast Process Ortho and Kodilith. Even when developed to their higher degree of contrast they maintain at the same time good resolving power (Fig. 5.2). In other words, the emulsion reproduces details very well, while sharply increasing contrast of weak strokes in relation to the paper background. Exposure and development normally follow manufacturer's recommendations, but other developers and exposures can be found with some experimentation. Tholl favors Kodilith for erased pencil writing both because of its contrast and its ability to reproduce fine detail. However, for this work he claims that a modified exposure and development with a moderate contrast developer, such as D-72, produces the best results.[2] Returning to the more common document copying films, the use of Contrast Process Panchromatic and Ektapan films on the same problem under identical lighting conditions produces two negatives of significantly different contrast. In some problems higher contrast can prove more successful, but in others the lower contrast can be more desirable. In all erasure problems preparation of negatives of more than one type is usually advantageous.

Figure 5.2. Modifications were made in an engineering drawing by erasing the original design. The arrows indicate weak traces of the original lines. This decipherment was recorded with Kodak Contrast Panchromatic Process film. The entire drawing was made with a relatively soft pencil that did not leave usable indentations but proved to be difficult to completely erase. Note the long pencil smudge in the upper left portion (indicated by arrow).

A method developed by the Kodak Laboratories is to expose Kodilith film normally and develop in the recommended solutions. However, development is by a "still bath" method. With tray development the film is throughly moistened with developer and agitated until the image begins to appear. At this point and until the completion of development by the time-temperature method there is no further agitation. Comparison of negatives made in this manner and those made with normal agitation throughout has shown that the "still bath" negative contains slightly greater detail.[3] The procedure can be used when confronted with partially erased, weak writing or when there are very slight graphite remains within the writing grooves. In actual case work this writer has experienced only limited success, but then no single method solves all cases.

Oblique Light Photographs

One of the standard means of deciphering erased pencil writing photographically is the use of oblique or low angle side lighting.[4] Whenever writing impressions remain from the original text this technique should be employed. The intensity of light and angle of incidence is an individual decision and governed by conditions of the problem at hand and personal experience. Choice of film is flexible, either moderate (Figs. 5.1 and 5.3) or high contrast emulsions (Fig. 5.4). The technique actually involves accentuating microscopic indentations by means of shadows and highlights. While one might utilize the method on an erasure in which there is no evidence of remaining writing grooves generally it has only minimum value. In practice after the lighting has been adjusted advantageously as judged visually, exposure and development should be controlled to give a sharp to high contrast negative.

As already indicated, the details of the method vary among workers. It does not mean that each method produces the same kind of photograph, but it is hoped that each produces an equally complete decipherment. Some prefer to use diffused daylight as a source of light, controlled by means of window blinds, and if needed, curtains or screens around the camera and copy. Others make these photographs entirely with incandescent lights, either by means of photofloods in appropriate reflectors or by means of spotlights (Fig. 5.5). The quality of daylight illumination may be extremely good, but on the other hand, the flexibility of incandescent lights and the ease of adjusting the angle of incidence of the light to the paper surface are strong recommendations for this kind of illumination. A fluorescent tube in efficient housing can also be used effectively,

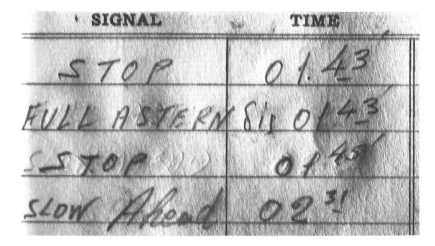

Figure 5.3. Erasure in a ship's engineroom log removed most of the graphite, but left pronounced indentations. They were recorded by photographing with a single floodlight directed at about a 30 degree angle to the paper surface. To right and left of the lower "STOP" are indentations of the lettered "SLOW AHEAD."

Figure 5.4. In a recount of a union presidential election these five ballots were found at the top of the ballot box. Erased crossmarks adjacent to the second candidate's name were revealed by oblique lighting and recorded with Kodak Contrast Panchromatic Process film developed to near maximum contrast.

although it is a softer light than incandescent light. Some photographs illuminated with fluorescent lights lack the contrast needed for the best negatives. Experience with each kind of illumination, however, can produce excellent results.

The most important consideration in making side light photographs is the angle at which the light strikes the paper. A light-paper angle of 10 to 30 degrees or occasionally less than 10 degrees produces the best results. The actual angle used may vary from problem to problem and depends on how flat the paper surface can be held and its texture. The best results are obtained if the paper is held flat without any cover glass. It is difficult to assure that the paper is absolutely flat unless one has a suction-type

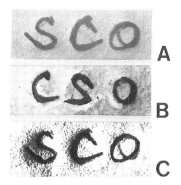

Figure 5.5. The chemist making a series of experiments used the letter CSO for cottonseed oil and SCO for 50 percent sulfated castor oil. Throughout his experimental records CSO had been changed to SCO, a key ingredient in a patent dispute. Section A is a photographic decipherment using low intensity oblique light. Section C is a photograph using a microscope spot illuminator as the source of low angle oblique lighting. In this instance irregular paper surface interfered with the decipherment of the "C" under the "S." Readjustment of the spotlight failed to improve the decipherment. The softer low intensity illumination proved somewhat superior. Section B is a low intensity photograph with the decipherable fragments traced in ink. The interferring overwriting has been obliterated by covering in Section A with white ink. This process will be found in several other illustrated decipherments.

copy board where atmospheric pressure holds the paper smooth. A simple box like unit with a perforated face on which the document rests can be evacuated by attaching a vacuum pump, even a home vacuum cleaner will do. Pages in account books and other types of record books are even more of a problem than single sheets, and here the ingenuity of the photographer often comes into full play. When the paper cannot be held absolutely flat, the angle of light incidence must be less oblique. A further consideration is the paper itself. Some rough textured papers are accentuated by low angle lighting, and with very oblique lighting paper fiber shadows are badly confused with weak indentations. Paper badly scuffed in the course of erasing creates similar problems. Resorting to a higher angle of incidence generally improves the results. Illumination directed from the top of the sheet, then the bottom, the right, then the left, suggested in Chapter 4 in the course of visual study, is equally effective for photographs.

A very useful device for side light photography is the oblique light box developed in the laboratories of the Royal Canadian Mounted Police.[5] In general its features include: A perforated base plate over a box from which the air can be evacuated by a vacuum pump, a light tight enclosure to shield the copy, and a movable top unit to the box that contains an adjustable slot opening and a light in suitable housing with baffles to provide for the low angle of oblique lighting. The document is placed over the perforated base plate and held fast by suction. The movable slot and light unit scans the document from top to bottom exposing successive stripes to the camera. The camera is mounted vertically above the unit, and the exposure is made with an open lens in a darkened room. Proper exposure is achieved by a series of uniform passes of the lighted slot. The top unit is moved manually or a motorized drive can be devised for this purpose, remembering that the motor must be reversable since the passes are back and forth. The unit provides for a high quality of oblique lighting and creates a balanced lighted negative. This last quality is a definite improvement over the somewhat unevenly illuminated negatives produced by a single light source photograph that has been traditional in these problems.

In making side light photographs it is always desirable to make two or more negatives rotating the copy in units of 45 or 90 degrees at a time. No single position can assure that all strokes will be at right angles to the direction of the light.

Vertical Illumination

Mathyer utilizes a technique for illumination with a light source and camera mounted vertically above the document.[6] His light source is a ring illuminator fit around the camera lens. This means that the light reflected from the document strikes the lens parallel to its axis. The document rests on a mirror, which slightly increases the reflected light. This arrangement improves the contrast between the reflecting areas and those in which there is absorption by the marking fragments. A green filter and contrast film with high gamma development are recommended for the best results. When using this lighting with a short focal length lens to photograph a single character at high enlargement, the light source will be close to the paper surface. This arrangement may cause the graphite fragments to shine and thus photograph at a comparable brightness to that of the white paper. The glare may be eliminated or weakened by the introduction of a polarizing filter for a satisfactory photograph. With badly distrubed paper surfaces vertical illumination also eliminates a good deal of the interference problems encountered with normal or oblique illumination.

ESDA

The ESDA (Electrostatic Detection Apparatus) is a electronic device that is highly sensitive to invisible writing pressures and impressions in paper. With pencil erasures the graphite is removed but writing impressions may remain, and by the same token the writing pressure pattern may be unharmed. Therefore, can the ESDA assist in developing what was originally written and erased?

The developers, D. J. Foster and D. J. Morantz,[7] describe the unit's operation as follows. The paper is placed on "an earthed, sintered metal vacuum bed" and covered with a sheet of insulating polymer film that is held tight by means of "suction applied through the sintered metal plate." The film is charged by a corona wire held above the sandwich and activated with a "potential of approximately 5kV." The surface potential on the film varies due to the differences in paper compression. The developed image can be recorded photographically or protected by a transparent adhesive sheet applied directly to the film.

When the ESDA was first developed it was subjected to a series of experimental problems, the results of which are reported by D. M. Ellen, J. D. Foster, and D. J. Morantz.[8] Ellen and subsequent workers have found that the ESDA can record very weak impressions in paper, even those that cannot be recorded by oblique lighting. Ellen continued his experimentation with the device. With erased pencil writing he was unsuccessful in revealing writing pressure traces either on the face or back of an erasure.[9] A few workers claim some success with deciphering pencil erasures. This writer in limited testing on erasures has not found the method helpful. With all types of problems both humidity and the type of paper can affect the results.[10] In the case of pencil erasures there remains a question concerning the usefulness of the ESDA. Tests are easy to perform and most workers consider that they leave the document unchanged. Tolliver recently demostrated that ESDA testing does remove a minimal amount of graphite from pencil writing.[11] Several decipherment methods depend on study of very weak graphite fragments, and if the ESDA test or even careless handling reduces the intensity of these fragments, chance of successful decipherment can be reduced.

Thus should one decide to run one, it may be well to wait until other attempted decipherments of the writing fragments have been completed.

When the erased document was originally written on a tablet and the undersheet is located, an ESDA test of the lower sheet may reveal evidence of the original writing. Similar results might be obtained from the following page of a notebook. However, with notebook writing it is not clear from the evidence at hand whether the erasing action on the upper page modifies the electrostatic differentials on the lower sheet that are needed for a successful ESDA determination.

Low Intensity Light

A further special lighting technique of value in deciphering erased pencil writing involves the use of low intensity illumination, especially with a daylight source.[12] It can be combined with the various types of photography already discussed. This procedure breaks with the more traditional approach of controlled strong lighting of the erased area.[13] Normally, high quality results are achieved with the copy set so that the weak light comes principally or exclusively from one side, but not necessarily at a very low oblique angle (Figs. 5.6 and 5.8B). Exposure is made on a moderate contrast film which is not developed to its maximum contrast. The most satisfactory light source is obtained with north daylight on a dull day. On brighter days a somewhat comparable intensity can be obtained with partially-closed blinds in order to extend the exposure time to between 10 and 20 times normal. The low contrast light source is well diffused and soft, but still tends to produce improved details over what is obtained with normal lighting. In making several such exposures it may be desirable to vary the angle of light incidence using low angle as well as moderate angles of incidence in order to emphasize any writing grooves that might remain from the original text. As with other directional lighting techniques, rotation of the copy for additional negatives is recommended.

Infrared Photographs

Infrared photography is one of the traditional ways of deciphering erased pencil writing.[14] Casual workers in the field seem to consider it *the* way. While it is a good technique, it is far from a cureall. It has been this writer's experience that very seldom do infrared photographs substantially improve on satisfactory decipherments by other photographic methods. Certain emulsions are specially sensitized to record some part of the invisible spectrum immediately beyond the visible red (in a range between 740 mu and 900 mu). When a document with pencil writing, or

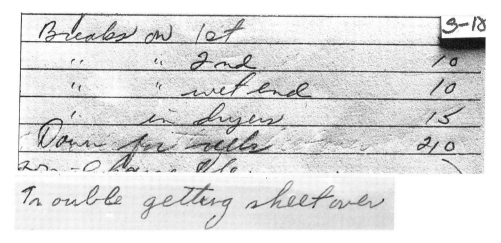

Figure 5.6. In a lawsuit against an equipment manufacturer a series of paper mill daily records were changed from the original causes of the paper machine shut down to "Down for reels." These changes attributed a great deal of lost time to the malfunctioning of the machine in question. With most altered records there were writing indentations of the original entry that could be deciphered by oblique lighting. In this decipherment low intensity illumination and Contrast Panchromatic Process film produced the best results. 210 is the number of minutes the paper machine was idle. Below is a tracing of the erased words, which were repeated in a number of other erased entries on other dates.

any marking substance containing carbon or other infrared absorbing constituents, is illuminated with an infrared rich light, the pencil writing absorbs the infrared radiation, while the balance of the document reflects greater quantities of it. Thus with partially erased fragments, the remaining carbon can be intensified by photographing with infrared film. The method has an advantage only if some unerased pencil traces remain on the paper.

The best illumination for infrared photography is a high wattage tungsten light or any other source rich in infrared. Fluorescent lights do not fulfill this requirement. Since all infrared films or photographic plates[15] are also sensitive to certain wavelengths of the visible spectrum, especially visible red and blue, either a deep red filter (Wratten 25, 29 or 92) or an infrared filter with very limited deep red sensitivity (Wratten 87 or 88A) is placed in the lens system. In this way only infrared and limited amounts of visible red radiation, reach the film.[16] Corning infrared filters, 7-57 and 7-56, have comparable transmission characteristics and are equally effective.

In order to maintain sharp focus when photographing using only the red and infrared spectrum a slight adjustment must be made in the film position. Focusing through a ground glass the focusing should be made with a red filter in place. Normally, this produces sharp negatives if the lens is stopped down even when using an infrared transmission filter. However, Tholl recommends a further adjustment in moving the film position an additional amount equal to the position difference between focus without a filter and with the deep red filter (Wratten 25) to obtain sharp focus for infrared transmission.[17] For most erasure decipherment photographs using infrared this latter step seems unnecessary as long as it is not necessary to photograph with the lens wide open.

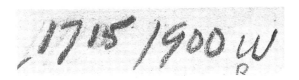

Figure 5.7. An infrared photograph of partially erased pencil reveals that the time group was originally 1710. The negative was made with a Kodak Spectroscopic Type N plate.

Exposing and developing infrared films to a moderately high contrast should produce a good photographic decipherment (Fig. 5.7). At times such photographs produce improved photographic decipherments compared to other techniques discussed in this chapter, but often results can be matched or bettered by other methods.

There is limited choice in infrared emulsions. Eastman Kodak is the sole domestic supplier. High speed infrared film is available in both 4 by 5 inch cut film and 35 mm roll film. Ektachrome infrared is also available in 35 mm rolls and requires E-4 processing. On special order infrared sensitive spectroscopic films and plates are available from Kodak. Type N films and plates have their peak sensitivity between 660 mu and 880 mu with somewhat weaker infrared sensitivity up to 920 mu and thus are suitable for erasure decipherment.[18] These plates produce high quality infrared decipherments (Fig. 5.7) but must be purchased in quantities that would limit their use to laboratories with high volume case work in problems requiring infrared photography. The commercially available high speed infrared film with proper development is a satisfactory film and when needed some additional contrast can be achieved by modifying exposure and development.

When black pencil erasures have been overwritten with ink (Fig. 5.8A) or colored pencil that is transparent to infrared, photographing with a

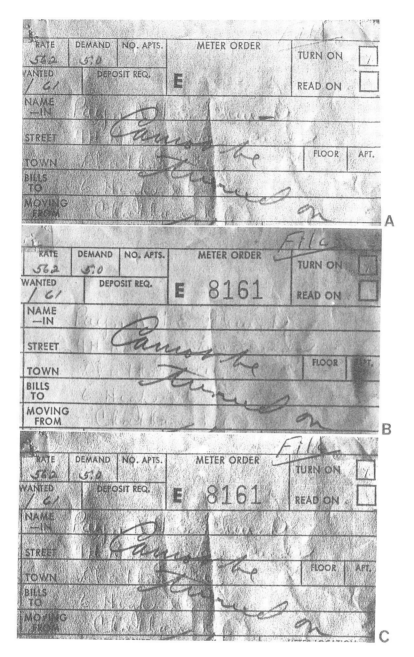

Figure 5.8. Three different photographic decipherments of an altered utility company's records are compared. The document was uncovered in a personnel investigation. Section A was prepared using Kodak Spectroscopic Type N plate. It recorded the ink written "File" as a clear indentation but, of course, did not weaken the pencil overwriting "Cannot be turned on." Section B was prepared with Contrast Panchromatic Process film and low intensity oblique illumination. The light source was on the left side of the copy. Section C was prepared with the same film but with low angle illumination using a single incandescent light on the left side of the copy. There is slightly more interference from the irregular paper surface in this photograph than in the low intensity photograph. However, some indented strokes are sharper in C than in B. Comparable development of the film was used for both negatives.

combination of infrared film and filter, such as Wratten 87 or 89B, is the recommended procedure. The photograph not only assists in deciphering what has been erased but eliminates or weakens the interferring overwriting (Fig. 5.9). This use is probably the most effective application of infrared photography in pencil erasure problems.

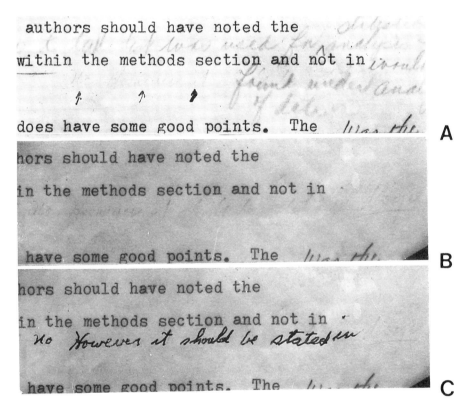

Figure 5.9. Comments on a typewritten critique. Two sets of handwritten, marginal comments appear throughout the document, one in red pencil, the other, in black. The unerased writing in section A is in red pencil. The arrows point to three partially erased words (black pencil) with evidence of additional erasures under the red writing, "found under analysis." Section B is a dark print of an infrared photograph of the writing (High Speed IR film with a Wratten 87 filter). This slightly intensified the fragments of black writing. In section C the decipherable writing fragments have been traced over to form the best interpretation of the original writing. The last word on the line could not be deciphered.

There is frequently advantage in employing infrared sensitive films with both normal and oblique lighting. The combination of oblique light and infrared may lead to decipherments not possible through other infrared techniques, and occasionally has improved upon standard oblique light photographs (Fig. 5.8). This type of photograph is particularly effective if some unerased pencil remains in the slight indentations from the expunged writing (Fig. 5.10).

It must be recognized that infrared films require special handling— preferably storage under refrigeration. The shelf life is less than standard emulsions. Holders and cameras must be infrared as well as light tight, and not all holders are. Thus, the use of these emulsions require special care.

In summary, infrared photographs are useful in deciphering erased pencil writing, but clearly superior only in limited cases where there is a need to eliminate overwriting with infrared transparent material. It is a method to use in conjunction with other procedures. Some moderate improvements may be obtained in certain problems with its use. However, in other cases results are no better or possibly somewhat inferior compared to the best decipherment that is derived by other photographic techniques. It should be pointed out that in comparing various decipherment techniques the difference may only be slight between the best result and those less satisfactory. In all probability, if only one method had been used a reasonable decipherment would be achieved in many cases. No clear-cut guidelines can be drawn from cases previously handled. Nevertheless, no incomplete or partial decipherment should be abandoned without preparing at least one infrared photograph.[19]

Filter Photography

Certain photographic filters may improve the decipherment of partially erased pencil writing. If the erased writing was written with a colored pencil rather than black, selection of a filter of contrasting color can intensify very weak fragments (Figs. 5.11 and 5.12A). If the overwriting in the erased area is in color rather than black, it can be weakened or eliminated by choosing a filter of similar color. For example, with an erasure of red pencil a green or blue filter helps to intensify the weak traces. If by chance the revised writing was made with a blue pencil, the blue would weaken the overwriting at the same time. Also with some colored pencils the proper choice of film emulsion characteristics, for example red or orange pencil photographed with a colorblind (blue sensitive) or ortho emulsion, leads to comparable results.

Pioneers in questioned document work recommended photographing pencil writing with a yellow filter (Wratten 8, K-2, or 9, K-3). These filters

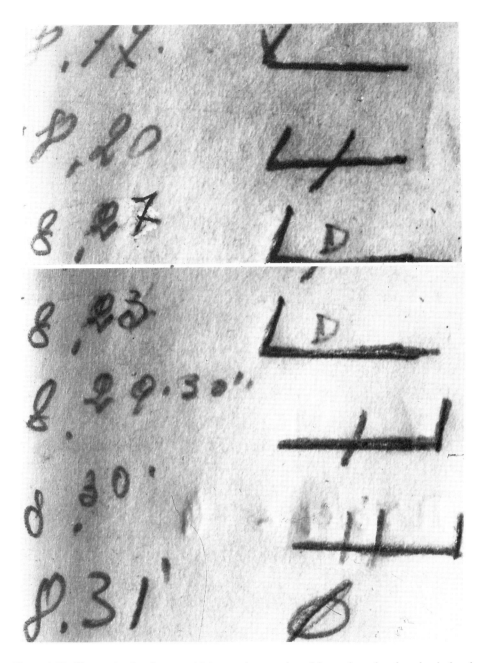

Figure 5.10. Change in the time at which speed was reduced from slow ahead to dead ahead was revealed by the combination of side lighting and infrared photography. Pencil writing in ship log books and other record books frequently contain significant writing indentations because of the relatively soft background of the following pages. With a partial erasure in which some graphite was not removed infrared can intensify the fragments somewhat (note in the 8.23 entry (lower section) the right end of the crossbar of the 7) and side lighting enhances the writing indentations. In the third entry, upper section, the "3" of the same 8.23 was obliterated and the fragments of the erased "7" traced in black. A four-minute change in ship maneuvering can be significant.

Figure 5.11. The partially erased date, written with a red pencil, was intensified using a green filter and panchromatic film. Rephotographing was also employed to further intensify the decipherment, July 24. (This evidence was examined prior to the introduction of infrared luminescence.)

may be of help today with modern emulsions in improving photographic decipherments of erased black pencil writing.

Infrared Luminescence

Infrared luminescence has limited application to the decipherment of pencil erasures but is of help in some problems. Since black pencil graphite does not luminesce, the method is of no assistance in deciphering this class of erasures. On the other hand, some, though not all, colored pencils have luminescence properties. Colored pencil writing is difficult to erase completely, and in a high percentage of cases some fragments persist. If the unerased writing displays luminescence, fragments of the erased writing may be more readily deciphered by infrared luminescence photography (Fig. 5.12B). Red pencils are probably the most commonly used of all colored pencils. At least 80 percent display some luminescence with better than 50 percent showing a bright recording (Fig. 5.13).[20] In event the writing does not luminesce, it becomes necessary to employ a series of standard decipherment procedures. By the same token, if after studying infrared luminescence photographs a complete decipherment is not obtained the document is completely unchanged, and all other nondestructive methods can still be employed.

In recent tests some red, orange, and yellow pencil writings have been found to produce a luminescence when viewed or photographed through a red filter under illumination by filtered ultraviolet radiation. Most of the same inks and pencils show no fluorescence when viewed directly under this illumination. Early work with the procedure suggests a high correlation between infrared luminescence and this red-ultraviolet luminescence. The test is simple to apply and under favorable condi-

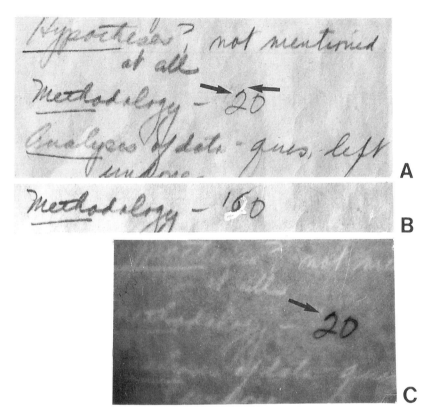

Figure 5.12. The document shown in Figure 5.9 contained these additional erasures. Section A is a portion of the concluding comments. The very dark "20" is black pencil written over erased red pencil (fragments marked by arrows). All writing in this illustration was intensified by photographing through a green (Wratten 58) filter. Section C is an infrared luminescence photograph (10% CuSO$_4$ light filter and High Speed IR film with Wratten 87 lens filter). The red pencil shows a moderate amount of bright luminescence, but only the weaken "1" can be distinguish in the erased area. Section B is a tracing of the best interpretation of the erasure, 16, based on a study of the two photographs and the original document. The interfering "2" of "20" was covered with white ink.

tions may aid in deciphering certain partially-erased red and orange writing.

Polaroid Screens

Experiments using Polaroid screens in deciphering erased writing indicates that their use is of limited value. The screen can be placed either over the camera lens or between the light source and the document. A pair of Polaroid screens, one over the lens and one on the light source,

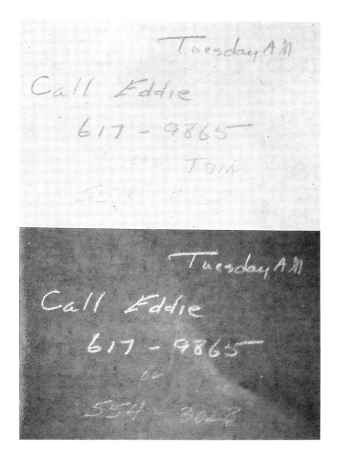

Figure 5.13. A telephone message pad contained a suggestion of an erased phone number beneath the unerased entry. All writing was with red pencil (upper section). The investigator questioned Tom who stated that he had written the entry with a single phone number during the conversation. An infrared luminescence photograph (lower section) revealed "or" above "544 - 3028." The notation "Tom" did not luminesce establishing it was written with a different pencil.

is sometimes more desirable. Rotating of one screen to reduce highlights shows slight improvement, but as a rule, this type of photograph offers no practical improvement unless one is dealing with an erasure on a glossy writing surface.

Processing Negatives

How negatives of erased writing are processed is certainly influenced by the individual's experience and preferences. Virtually all examiners have adopted solutions that they routinely use and favor. For the most part they are to be recommended in preference to some specific solution. Still it is well to investigate other developers, especially those of higher contrast in order to be able to use them effectively. Familiarity with a developer and how negatives can be manipulated with it to control contrast and density generally leads to better results than using a special developer only occasionally. Preparing two negatives with the same film, one processed normally and the second with modified exposure and development to increase contrast, may be all that is needed to reach a final decipherment. On the other hand, a single developer may not always produce the best results. There is always a need in these problems to be on the lookout for improved processing methods.

Some workers prefer using a high contrast developer, but it is important to handle contrast so that there is a minimum of loss of detail. A developer that produces good detail but only moderate contrast can lead to a substantial decipher showing that detail is as important in photographic decipherments as contrast. Tholl, for example, used D-72 developer with Kodalith film rather than the standard high contrast developer to produce negatives with fine detail.[21]

In preparing positives from good negatives glossy finished papers are to be preferred. Various contrasts should be used as well as slightly different densities in a set of prints. From these the best reproduction can be chosen. Differences encountered from problem to problem means that no single grade of paper is always going to produce the most complete decipherment. Workers will find that only with a partial erasure, in which most of the original writing can be read without any special equipment, is it possible to achieve a complete decipherment from a single negative and print. With erasure problems several negatives of slightly different quality and a series of prints from these is often the best procedure to assure success.

Improving Contrast

There are cases in which the best available negative does not record all the details with sufficient contrast to interpret them accurately. Some improvement in contrast is indicated. One technique is to treat the negative with Farmer's reducer until it is significantly reduced followed by intensification with a proportional intensifier. Some improvement in the negative may be achieved by the process, and the prints should show greater contrast.

Some increase in the contrast of the final print may be achieved without loss of detail by first preparing a good quality print and rephotographing it. Care must be taken that detail is not lost by too much contrast. Some experience in rephotographing other types of document photographs, as for example, copying an assembled group of field photographs to make a justaposition court exhibit, can be utilized so that excessive contrast is avoided and significant detail is not lost (Fig. 5.14).

Color Films

To date very little has been reported on concerning decipherment of erased pencil writing using color films. There is no apparent advantage with erasure of black pencils, but examiners who use these films frequently may find methods for producing satisfactory decipherments. Godown reports good results with writing indentations by photographing in normal room illumination and placing an electronic flash so as to provide a low angle light beam.[22] An examiner who processes his own film might experiment with variations in development to intensify the photograph recognizing that color balance might be unsatisfactory. With weak, partially-erased writing that was prepared with a colored pencil these films may produce a decipherment as effectively as black and white photography.

Superimposed Negatives

The use of multiple negatives provides a further special technique. Two or more duplicate negatives are prepared. Each is made under identical conditions of enlargement and exposure, with exposure controlled to produce a thin negative. The negatives are carefully superimposed in exact register and prints prepared. The procedure is known to result in a print containing somewhat more information than can be obtain by other means.

An alternative provides for the partial elimination of interfering overwriting. A positive transparency is made from an ordinary negative of the erased area without any attempt to intensify the partially-erased fragments. It is superimposed in register with a negative of identical enlargement containing the best photographic decipherment that can be achieved. The combined positive and negative image of the interferring overwriting weakens this portion of the resulting print, while the fragments of erased writing are printed from the decipherment negative without significant loss of detail. Skillful balancing of positive and negative images can lead to decipherments that are difficult to obtain from a single negative of the suspected area.[23]

Back of Document

With many pencil written documents containing an erasure, both the original and the new overwriting leave impressions in the paper. If the back of the sheet is blank, and sometimes even with limited writing behind the erasure, a better decipherment may be obtained by photographing that side for study. The embossings are recorded and emphasized by carefully controlled, oblique light photography. Any of the methods of side lighting already discussed should give good results. The use of ESDA recording should also be considered. In order to facilitate interpretations of the writing the negative is printed from its reverse side, thus correcting the mirror image of the writing impressions. While the impressions of the overwriting may also be recorded, the two, erased and unerased, are nearly equal in intensity so that both may be read with equal ease. It is relatively simple to interpret what belongs to the erased text (Fig. 5.14c). In contrast, a comparable photograph of the face of the sheet finds the unerased overwriting dominating (Fig. 5.14A).

SUMMARY

Before attempting any photographic decipherment techniques, some preliminary examination must be made. This examination plus experience with these problems generally suggest the most suitable photographic procedure. If a single method leads to complete decipherment, all is well. However, in the majority of instances the first photograph may seem to lack some qualities of a perfect decipherment. Other techniques are generally tried. With most problems, if time permits, more than one photograph ought to be made. In this way decipherments from the first can be verified from the second. Preparing photographs to decipher erasures requires an experimental approach (Fig. 5.15c), and it has been this writer's experience that no single procedure is apt to

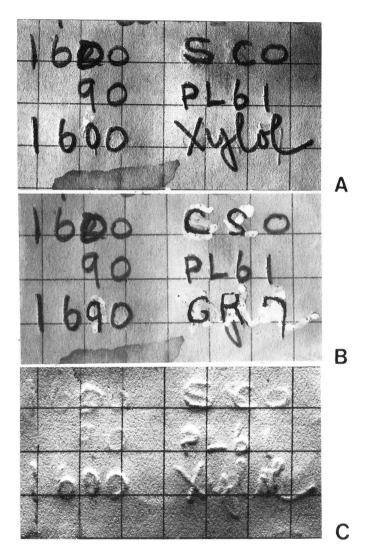

Figure 5.14. Another change in the research chemist's notes involving formula changes from CSO to SCO (see Fig. 5.5). Further changes occurred in the last line with Xylol written over an erased GR 7. Indentations of the original writing are revealed in section A by an oblique light photograph of the face of the document. In section C (the back of the sheet) the indentations of both sets of writings are shown as raised embossing. The traced "CS" and "GR 7" in section B were derived by detailed study of both photographs. (Xylol was covered by white ink.) Photographs of the back of a document frequently assists in interpreting writing impressions of erasures.

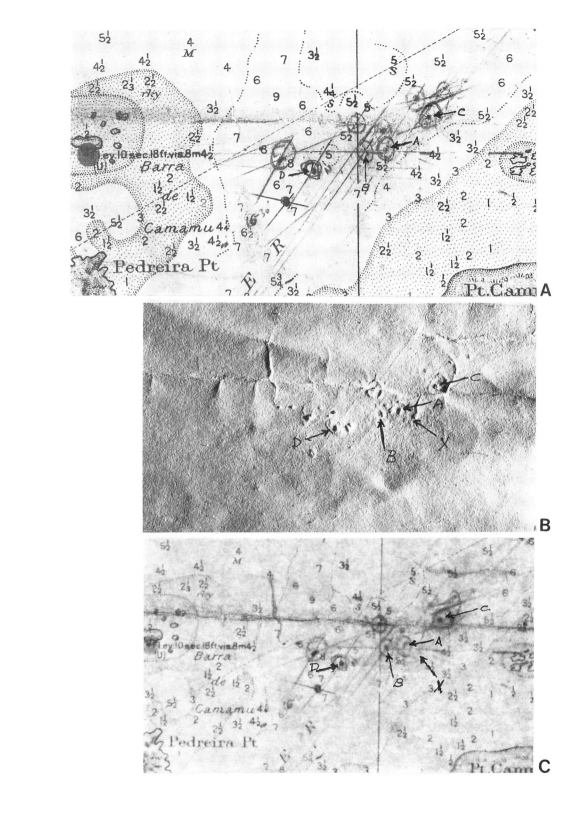

Figure 5.15. Section A is a portion of the Camanu harbor chart showing successive position of the Atlantic Oriole. She was outward bound, loaded and proceeding in a generally northeast direction when she grounded at point A. According to the captain she was successfully backed off to point B. She then proceeded to point C where she again grounded. The second grounding was serious and the ship was only refloated at high tide and anchored at point D. Inspection of the chart raised a suspicion of alterations since the point C, the second grounding, was not located on the chart by crossed bearing lines that fixed every other position.[25] In searching for possible erased positions marks the back of the chart was photographed under oblique lighting (section B). Embossing of position points and some course and bearing lines were revealed. However, it is not easy to interpret location of key points that have been marked with arrows. (The photograph was printed from the reverse side of the negative in order to relate the points in proper left-right position to those on the face of the chart. This procedure causes raised embossing to appear as indentations.) Section C is a combined transmitted light and side light photograph of the back of the chart. It records the marking on the chart itself but with the embossing on the back, slightly less intense. The print was also made from a reversed negative. The arrow X on this and the other photographs locates an erased position and further study of the chart revealed partially erased bearing lines to fix its position. Point X is in shallow water (5 fathoms) where the loaded ship would have grounded. This and other points are established by the intersection of the line from the flashing light (large black circle on the left edge of the chart, section A), and the bearing of a pier head (not shown in section A.

produce a complete decipherment. Certainly, no one method is the best for every problem, even those with many similar elements.

Photography is a virtually indispensible method for deciphering erased pencil writing. But it is far from an automatic tool. With skill, experience, and perseverance, however, it has proven in many cases to reveal most completely what was originally written and subsequently erased.

Notes

1. Godown, Linton: Faint Document Evidence (unpublished). Read at 1984 meeting, American Society of Questioned Document Examiners.
2. Tholl, Joseph: Uses of Kodalith film in the examination of questioned documents. *PSA Journal, Photographic Science and Technique, 19B,* 1952, 96.
3. Rudd, G, Eastman Kodak Laboratories, Rochester, NY, described the procedure to member of the American Society of Questioned Document Examiners in 1951, and correspondence with Harris Tuttle of Kodak concerning its use.
4. Ames, Daniel T.: *Ames on Forgery,* New York, Ames-Rollinson, 1900, p. 270.
5. Duxbury, N. W. and Warren, J. W.: Deciphering and Photo-Recording of Indented Writing. *RCMP Laboratories, Seminar no. 4, Examination of Questioned Documents,* 1956, 27.
6. Mathyer, J.: Photography and the police, part 2. *International Criminal Police Review,* No. 256, 1972, 73.
7. Foster, D. J. and Morantz, D. J.: An electrostatic imaging technique for the

detection of indented writing impressions in documents, *Forensic Science International, 13,* 1979, 51.

8. Ellen, D. M., Morantz, D. J. and Foster, D. J.: The use of electrostatic imaging in the detection of indented impressions. *Forensic Science International, 15,* 1980, 53.
9. Ellen, David M.: Some thoughts on ESDA, (unpublished). Read at 1982 meeting, American Society of Questioned Document Examiners.
10. Noblett, Michael G. and James, Elizabeth L.: Optimum conditions for examination of documents using an electrostatic apparatus (ESDA) device to visualize indented writings. *J Forensic Sciences 28,* 1983, 697.
11. Tolliver, Diane K.: The electrostatic detection apparatus (ESDA): is it really non-distructive to documents? *Forensic Science International* (in press).
12. Hilton, Ordway: Photographic methods of deciphering erased pencil writing. *International Criminal Police Review,* no. 85, 1955, 47.
13. Ames (see note 4) first suggested the use of strong, side or oblique light as a means of reading erased pencil writing grooves.
14. Waters, Louis A.: Further experiments in infrared. *Camera* (Philadelphia), *34,* 1934, 233. (Cited by Clark, Walter: *Photography in Infrared,* New York, Wiley, 1964, p. 354. Radley, J. R.: *Photography in Crime Detection,* London, Chapman-Hall, 1948, p. 157–158, also cites Waters, *Camera* (Philadelphia) *47,* 1933, 361; *48,* 1934, 18 and *American Photography, 33,* 1937, 336.)
15. Infrared sensitive plates are available on special order from Kodak, some with infrared sensitivity beyond that of Kodak High Speed Infrared film. They must be purchased in quantity and require at least 90 days for delivery.
16. Based on experimental work by this writer, results are not improved by using infrared filters that pass only infrared radiation or infrared and visible radiation beyond 800 mu. For erased pencil decipherment deep red filters, such as Wratten 25 and 29, are probably as effective as Wratten 87 or other infrared filters.
17. Tholl, Joseph: Infrared photography of documents. *PSA Journal, Photographic Science and Techniques, 17B* 1951 34.
18. See note 15 for availability.
19. Hilton, Ordway: Reapparaising infrare photography's worth in deciphering erased writing. *J Criminal Law, Criminology and Police Science, 57,* 1966 368.
20. These figures are based on a review of infrared luminescence recording of 43 red pencils produced in this country and Europe. They represent different tints of red. Of the group 35 pencils displayed some luminescence, 24 of them bright. A more detailed analysis of these pencils and other colored pencils can be found in: Ordway Hilton: Identification and differentiation between colored pencils. *Forensic Science, 6,* 1975, 221. With blue, green, and yellow pencils a very few showed even weak luminescence.
21. See note 2, p. 96.
22. See note 2
23. Gayet, Jean: A method of superimposed photography applied to criminalistics. *J Criminal Law, Criminology and Police Science, 44,* 1953, 388.
24. Panatomic-X sheet film was used for these photographs. Some years ago Ektapan

replaced it. With this latter film and careful processing comparable results are obtained.

25. When cruising within confined waters, such as a harbor, the ship's position is determined by taking bearings from two fixed objects, that is determining the angle of sight relative to the ship's heading. Such object must be accurately positioned on the chart so that lines from them fix the position of the ship. It is customary to draw lines on the chart in pencil, and to erase the earlier record and to reuse the chart. In this case several other positions are noted in the area of the chart under consideration and probably represent positions plotted on the inbound trip or an earlier visit to this port.

Chapter 6

CHEMICAL METHODS OF DECIPHERMENT

E rased pencil writing does not lend itself to chemical decipherments. Most problems involve an ordinary black pencil. The marking substance, as has been pointed out earlier, is graphite, a form of carbon. There are no chemicals that react with graphite to assist in deciphering what was erased. In fact a complete erasure removes all the carbon particles deposited during the writing process. The original pencil writing consisted of graphite that was entirely on the paper surface, or at best wedged between the fibers. No chemical penetrates the fibers, so no invisible substance remains after erasing. With colored pencil writing the marking substance consists of dry dyes and lakes that are attached to the paper in the same manner as graphite. There is no fiber penetration by these dry marking materials either. Thus, if completely erased, again nothing remains that can be treated chemically to assist in deciphering the erasure. To summarize simply, there are no reagents that can combine with any unremoved or invisible marking substance to bring about a chemical decipherment.

There are available, however, a limited number of chemical methods that are of some assistance. They depend on the compression of the paper fibers for success. One method is simply to fume the paper surface with iodine, which accumulates more rapidly along the writing impressions, and thus reveals evidence of the original writing in the form of a deeper color. A slightly more effective method involves the use of a staining solution made up principally of iodine that is absorbed into the paper fibers differently where they have been compressed than where they have not.

Iodine Fuming

The best procedure for fuming the document with iodine is to suspend it in a closed container which is saturated with iodine fumes. The ideal container is a box with a glass front and back in which the paper can be hung vertically. A shallow dish of iodine crystals is placed on the floor of the box. With this arrangement the atmosphere gradually becomes saturated with iodine. Saturation can be hastened by heating the crystals. A convenient heating unit is a small light bulb placed under the iodine dish.[1] The document is hung so that it can be inspected through the glass front and removed as soon as the impressions from the pressure writing have been developed to a reasonable degree of legibility. Lucas suggests giving attention to the back of the sheet in this process.[2]

The method is far from foolproof; in some instances it does not work well at all. The document may become stained from the fumes, and yet no erased writing develops even though indentations can be seen. If the document has been recently handled, iodine will likely develop latent fingerprints. They can seriously interfere with the study of writing traces. Other stains may develop and also interfere.[3] The disturbed paper fibers, resulting from the erasing action, may cause blotchy staining in critical areas. While the chemical action is normally reversible, a yellow residue stain from the iodine is known to remain on the paper for several days after treatment.

When the technique is successful the sheet takes on a reddish brown color with the erased writing outline more intense than the rest of the sheet. The method can also be applied to the development of writing impressions on a blank sheet of paper in which the embossings were impressed by writing on the sheet above. A somewhat better chance of success may be expected, but the same limitations apply. (See Chapter 8 for further discussion of the problem.)

Differential Staining Solutions

There are several staining solutions that can be used to develop pressure traces in paper. The solutions are compounds of iodine and halogen salts and depend on differential physical absorption rather than chemical reaction for success. A reagent developed by Joseph Ehrlich, patented by the now expired U. S. patent 2123597, consists of two solutions that are combined before application to the paper.

	Solution A
200 gm.	magnesium chloride
100 gm.	water
	Solution B
40 gm.	potassium chloride
0.15 gm.	iodine
40 cc	water

Other workers have used modifications of this formula. Rhodes published a slightly different formula that produces comparable results.[4]

4 gm.	potassium iodine
0.1 gm.	iodine
5 gm.	sodium chloride
2 gm.	aluminum chloride
3.5 gm.	glycerine
30 cc	water

Rhodes warns that the solution must be prepared with caution since if aluminum chloride is added too rapidly it produces a violent reaction. The solution should be kept cool while the chemical is added slowly.

The erasing process normally roughens the paper surface slightly and loosens the fibers. Thus, the erased area may be overly absorbent and acts like a blotter. The staining solution in these cases may be applied with a cotton swab to the undisturbed back of the sheet. If traces of erased writing are developed, they can be photographed, and the image reversed in printing for easy reading. When using the technique, one must be prepared to photograph the document promptly since the developed writing fades rather rapidly. The method requires some skill of manipulation. Whenever possible, the solution should be pretested on similar paper since some papers can absorb the solution rapidly before any decipherment develops. Further the liquid may seriously damage the impressions. After recording the decipherment, the residue stain can be removed by swabbing with a simple hypo solution.

One further precaution—unless one has developed a high proficiency with the technique, it is well to try ESDA and visual and photographic methods first in order to record the most complete decipherment obtainable by these methods. Unsuccessful results from the application of the solution can seriously limit subsequent examination by weakening the indentations or staining the paper. Successful chemical decipherment is dependent on the presence of some paper compression from the erased writing. If preliminary study of the document indicates that the document was written with light writing pressure, there is only a slight probability that the treatment will be successful. If writing embossing is suggested, the method should be of help, but standard examinations, especially oblique light examinations and photography, and possibly the ESDA, can be effective and are safer.

Developing Iron Impurities

Harrison suggests chemical intensification of partially erased pencil writing may be accomplished by means of testing for iron impurities.[5] Since these impurities represent at best a small part of the deposit, very sensitive reagents need to be used. A highly sensitive iron reagent is thiocyanic acid that reacts with low concentrations of iron forming a red brown reaction. Development of iron traces can be effected by fumes produced by treating potassium thiocyanate crystals with dilute hydrochloric acid (5%).[6] A liquid solution of thiocyanic acid can be sprayed on the document with a nebulizer rather than fuming.[7] With the same technique the more sensitive Yoe's iron reagent (Tiron) develops the weak iron as a blue stain.[8] Even if iron is present in the pencil writing, it is in solid form like the graphite. When all of the graphite has been erased, the chances of iron impurities remaining is remote. Thus the method appears to have limited application. In those instances that this writer has tried, thiocyanic acid fumes results were all negative.

Alcohol Spray

Copy pencils are used very infrequently today. If erased writing was prepared with one, it can be subjected to special chemical treatment. These pencils, as is well known, contain an aniline dye ground and mixed with the graphite. When moistened the dye gives the characteristic purple or blue color of the "indelible" pencil stroke. With a partial erasure, the die fragments, which may be present, can still be developed by use of an aerosol spray of alcohol.[9] The light, moist film is not apt to damage the paper by staining or weakening the indentations when no dye is developed.

Conclusions

The circumstances surrounding a case may mitigate against chemical treatment. Restrictions on what tests are to be used can be imposed by those who control the document and even confirmed by a court. With some documents there are not these restrictions. The need for developing every fact contained in the document can far outweigh the desire to preserve the paper in the same conditions as when discovered. In other words, discoloration from only partially successful chemical treatment is not a matter of paramount concern. Chemical tests may occasionally reveal facts no other method will. It certainly should be considered in problems in which other tests have failed. At times chemical tests may lead to a complete decipherment, but more likely, if of any value, may merely reveal additional information to that which earlier methods have achieved.

Notes

1. To construct a simple iodine fuming cabinet see: Scott, Walter R.: *Fingerprint Mechanics.* Springfield, Thomas, 1951, Section 132, p. 248.
2. Lucas, A.: *Forensic Chemistry and Criminal Investigation,* 4th ed., London, Arnold, 1946, p. 94.
3. The use of iodine fumes to reveal erased areas was discussed in Chapter 3. As pointed out the action of the rubber eraser and the fumes combine to create a dark discoloration in the erased area.
4. Rhoads, H. T. F.: *Forensic Chemistry.* New York, Chemical Publishing, 1940, p. 135.
5. Harrison, Wilson R.: *Suspect Documents.* New York, Praeger, 1958, p. 215.
6. The original use of thiocyanic acid fumes is reported by O'Neill, M. E.: Restoration of obliterated ink writing. *J. Criminal Law and Criminology, 27,* 1936 p. 574, in connection with the restoration of erased iron base inks.
7. Longhetti, A. and Kirk, P. L.: Restoration and decipherment of erased and obliterated or indented writing. *J. Criminal Law and Criminology, 41,* 1950, p. 518.
8. Yoe's iron reagent (disodium-1, 2-dihydroxybenzene-3, 5-disulfonate) is another highly sensitive reagent for revealing the presence of iron. It was sold in the 1950's by LaMott Chemical Company, Chestertown, Maryland, as Tiron. Hilton, Ordway: Evaluation of chemical methods for restoring erased ink writing. *The Police Journal* (England), *29,* 1956, p. 264. The reaction of the solution of 0.1g Tiron in 5cc water and a buffer solution of 1.0g sodium bicarbonate and 0.5g sodium carbonate in 100cc water is the most highly sensitive of all iron reagents. (Fegl, F.: *Qualitative Analysis by Spot Tests,* New York, Elsevier, 1947, p. 126.)
9. See note 7, p. 519.

Chapter 7

PHYSICAL METHODS OF DECIPHERMENT

Several decipherment techniques involving physical intensification of the erased writing have been suggested. They involve methods of making the original writing impressions on the paper clearer or of transferring the indentations to a plastic material where they can be studied further and more readily. The former techniques include dusting with fingerprint or fluorescent and other powders and of simply "aging the sheet." These processes are far from universally successful, but they do merit consideration.

Dusting with Powders

Fine powder dusted or shaken across the surface of the paper tend to accumulate in the writing grooves and fiber crevices. When they settle in the impressions from the erased writing, they clarify the outline of these traces. Some latent fingerprint powders are suitable for this purpose. Black powders, made of finely divided carbon particles, contrast sharply with the white paper, but a number of other colored materials used in fingerprint work are also available.[1] Some workers prefer fluorescent powders that in ordinary light are similar to the paper in color, but under ultraviolet radiation fluoresce in a sharp contrast to the paper. The bright fluorescence of anthracene serves effectively if the paper has a dark hue under ultraviolet radiation. Ultraviolet absorbent or dark fluorescent powders should be selected if the paper contains fluorescent brightner and appears nearly white under ultraviolet.[2]

Regardless of type, the powder is sprinkled lightly on the paper and shaken across the suspected erased area. The powder can also be dusted over the area, if preferred, with a light camel hair, fingerprint dusting brush. After the powder is deposited in the writing grooves the surplus should be removed from the paper. The results can then be studied visually or photographically.

When fluorescent powders are used, examination and photography must be carried out in a darkened room under filter ultraviolet radiation. The fact that these powders do not discolor the paper surface the way the colored fingerprint powders do is their chief advantage, especially when results are negative or fragmentary.

The principal shortcomings of the dusting method is the lack of consistent results. Furthermore, there is a limited number of instances in which it seems appropriate to try the technique. Application of powders soils or discolors the area and hinders other tests. It is only successful when writing indentations are present. But roughed paper surfaces with disturbed paper fibers as well as writing indentation tend to catch and accumulate the powder.[3] Since it requires extensive rubbing with an eraser to create writing indentations devoid of graphite, such action is almost sure to lead to a marked disturbance of the paper surface. These conditions may restrict the value of the technique and suggest that some other method should be employed.

Lucas suggests dusting or staining the writing embossings on the back of the sheet. Of course it must be recognized that the embossings probably are not as intense as the indentations since the paper tends to be compressed slightly, but they should be present if the indentations occur on the face of the sheet. Treatment of the reverse side avoids the rough, erased surfaces and may lead to somewhat better results.[4] Certainly, any residue powders will not interfere with the majority of other tests.

Shading with Pencil

Indentations from erased writing can be developed by rubbing the paper surface around the erasure with the flat side of a soft pencil lead. The nondepressed paper surface is darkened, while the indentations stand out in relief as light grooves. *This method should not be used.* The treatment badly defaces the document and results can be extremely unreliable. However, the most significant objection is that the method defaces the paper with the identical substance that was originally erased. If it becomes necessary, because of failure of the test, to clear off the added graphite, it must be thoroughly erased, a process that is certain to take off some, if not all, of the remaining graphite from the original writing. Other pencil writing on the document is likewise apt to be damaged. The end results may well leave the document in worse condition than before treatment.

Plastic Replicas

Longhetti and Kirk have suggested preparation of a plastic replica from the writing indentations.[5] The paper with the erased writing is placed on a soft backing such as a tablet. A sheet of thermoplastic is superimposed over the writing indentations and glass placed on top. The plastic and the paper are held in tight contact by means of weights set around the edge of the glass outside the erased area. With an infrared heat lamp hung over the assembly, the plastic is heated until it just begins to flow. The heat source is removed, and the pressure maintained on the glass until the thermoplastic resets. When the paper is separated from the plastic, the plastic sheet should contain an accurate cast of the writing impression left from the erased writing indentations.

The originators of the technique indicate excellent results. However, this author and others do not entirely agree. In some instances the results are satisfactory; however, on occasion serious difficulty has been encountered in separating the paper from the cast resulting in some damage to the paper itself.

The originators maintain correctly that if the indentations can be transferred to the plastic, they may be studied more effectively from the replica than from the original, especially in cases where there is interfering overwriting. While the need for this method is encountered only infrequently, it is another useful technique that can assist with deciphering the impressions of the erased writing and typewriting.

Other Replicas

Thorpe suggests preparing a replica of the impressions from erased writing and other sources with silicone rubber.[6] He prefers Dow Corning Silastic 585 RTV silicone rubber. The required amount of 585 RTV is poured in a mixing bowl, a few drops of 502 Catalyst are added. The mixture is stirred thoroughly and spread over the area of the document in question. Cure or hardening time is governed by the amount of catalyst and temperature. A thin layer of rubber is spread around each indentation, pressing out all air bubbles. When all bubbles are worked out, a second layer of rubber is spread over the area and a piece of paper towelling is placed on top of the last layer. A slow set may take as long as an hour to an hour and one-half. When the cast is removed, it is dusted with a silver grey fingerprint powder for increased viewing contrast or photographing. Some examiners prefer to omit the dusting step and examine or photograph the clear cast. General Electric also produces a high quality silicone rubber paste, RTV 77, and a more fluid RVT 11, that should give comparable results.

Leung and Tang[7] recommend the use of Mikrosil,[8] a Swedish product, for casting impressions in a variety of documents such as credit cards and passports. Its applications can be extended to the problem at hand. Setting time of the material can be varied from a few minutes to an hour depending on temperature and the amount of hardener used.

Aging

The apparent legibility of writing impressions from an erasure has been known to improve slightly in the course of several days of intermittent examinations. The phenomenon has been observed by the writer in a number of cases and confirmed by others. Any development by this technique apparently results from accumulation of fine dust particles in the microscopic indentations. In other words, this aging may be a slow, natural powder dusting technique in which only microscopic amounts of dust are involved. The writer is not advocating or suggesting by these statements that the sheet should be deliberately soiled, but rather he is only attempting to rationalize the cause of improved legibility. While the limited change may assist in deciphering what was erased, the condition does not necessarily lead to a full, automatic decipherment.

SUMMARY

To repeat what has already been commented on at several points, decipherment of erasures may depend on combining fragments of several examinations. Physical decipherment techniques rarely reveal fully what has been erased, but this does not mean that the technique should be discredited. However, it no doubt should be applied more frequently than it actually is, recognizing it chiefly as supplementary methods. Furthermore, whenever these methods might deface the document, and thus restrict other examinations, they must be postponed until late in the technical investigation. Recognizing such limitations, certain cases will be encountered in which knowledge of the method and experience with its use may result in a more complete decipherment.

Notes

1. Readers unfamiliar with fingerprint powders and methods for applying them should refer to standard texts on latent fingerprint development. A useful text is: Moenssens, Andre A.: *Fingerprnt Techniques,* 1971, Philadelphia, Chilton.
2. Several additional methods, which were developed for deciphering indented writing, may also be applied to writing impressions from erased pencil writing. See Chapter 8 for specific discussion.
3. Refer to Chapter 3 for Harrison's method of detecting areas of the paper disturbed by erasing in which he used these powders.
4. Lucas, A.: *Forensic Chemistry and Criminal Investigation,* 4th ed., London, Arnold, 1946, p. 94.
5. Longhetti, A. and Kirk, P. L.: Restoration and decipherment of erased and obliterated or indented writing. *J. Criminal Law, Criminology and Police Science, 41,* 1950, 519.
6. Thorpe, W. D.: The use of silicone rubber by the document examiner. *J. Forensic Sciences, 16,* 1971, 530.
7. Leung, S. C. and Tang, M. M. H.: The application of half-silved mirror in conjunction with casting techniques to document examination. *Forensic Science International, 45* 1990, 63.
8. Carlsson, K.: A new casting material for forensic use. *International Criminal Police Review,* no. 346, 1981, 74.

Chapter 8

DECIPHERMENT OF IMPRESSED WRITING

IMPRESSED VS ERASED WRITING

Closely related to the problems of deciphering erased writing are those that involve writing impressions. These impressions are embossed in the paper by writing pressure from the sheet above. Normally, most impressions are found on tablet paper or pages of a record book where the original writing was prepared on the previous sheet or at times one or two sheets above it (Fig. 8.1). Writing impressions are also encountered in bound documents when, for example, they are executed after assembly or from alterations or changes made after the document was assembled. Such almost invisible writing traces may be of potential or sufficient importance to warrant the often extended study necessary to achieve a decipherment.[1]

Writing impressions are an important consideration in deciphering erasures of pencil. Now, however, some writing impressions occur in areas where there have been no erasures. In such problems the examiner must determine whether the impressions have been transmitted from a sheet that rested on the document during the former's preparation or whether the impressions are the result of erasing previous writing on the sheet under study. When there has been an erasure the indentations are commonly accompanied with disturbances or changes in the paper surface. Graphite fragments may also be present around the impressions (Fig. 8.2). If, on the other hand, the writing impressions are from another document, the indentations and the area around them will not contain typical evidence of erasing. Except for the slight writing grooves the surrounding paper contains no fragments of graphite or paper disturbances (Fig. 8.3). In some instances the groove edges are not as sharp and pronounced as those typical of erased pencil writing.

Because of the relationship between the decipherment of erased pencil writing and writing impressions and especially because the latter are encountered in a certain number of erased pencil writing problems, it is

Figure 8.1. Impressed writing found in a tablet sheet. An oblique light photograph of this page revealed only trivial matter, as can be seen readily in the right section where the strokes have been traced in ink. Other documents in the case produced more helpful information. Note also the weaker impression below "walk" in the first line and at a few other points on the sheet, apparently from the second or third page above this one.

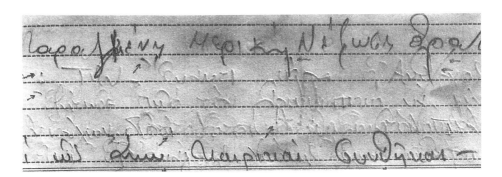

Figure 8.2. These strong writing impressions in a Greek ship's log were believed to be part of an erased entry. Or were they writing impressions from some other page of document? Proof that it was an erasure is based primarily on the small fragments of unerased pencil carbon, some of which are indicated by arrows. Note also the weakening of the second from the right long downstroke below line one and the base of some other letters in the same area above the ruled line.

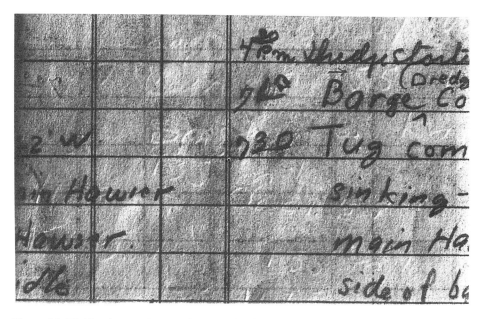

Figure 8.3. Writing impressions on the page of a ship's log were improperly interpreted as part of an erased entry. Actually they were writing indentations from another sheet as it rested on this book. The strokes are devoid of carbon deposits. Further some writing is found in columns of the book that were not used on any other page. In the case of the indented "55" above "Barge" (line 2, right), as well as other parts of the impressed writing, these strokes appear between ruled lines not on them and are not always parallel to the rulings. Partial decipherment suggested that the ship's position and other data of the voyage had been transcribed to another sheet.

appropriate at this time to reconsider the techniques that might be applied to deciphering these impressions. Any method that has previously been discussed in connection with deciphering erased pencil writing and that can intensify or make more visible the remaining indentations of the original writing can be immediately adapted to the problem at hand. Today a very efficient means of reading writing impressions or pressure traces is to record them with the ESDA (Electrostatic Detection Apparatus).

ESDA

The ESDA is a highly sensitive device that prepares a positive photocopy of writing impressions or pressure patterns on a sheet that had rested beneath another document during its preparation.[2] It is very effective with writing impressions, having the capacity of developing writing that is virtually invisible under visual or other photographic methods.[3] Thus, it is the recommended first test.

Normally, the ESDA develops pressure patterns efficiently. However, if the paper is tested under very dry conditions, results can be poor or even negative. To overcome this early researchers recommended the document's pretreatment in a humidity chamber.[4] The Metropolitan Police Forensic Science Laboratory, London, found that even with this pretesting treatment, ESDA results dropped appreciably with a drop in room humidity. To overcome this problem they designed a controlled humidity room for ESDA testing (70% relative humidity) with a substantial increase in successful decipherments.[5]

Documents containing strong visible writing impression may record poorly with the ESDA while under sheets give adequate results. With the rather clear impressions, however, they may be deciphered using traditional visual and photographic techniques. There is another possible limitation. The machine design may interfere with the testing of bound documents if the sheets in question cannot be removed. Here again other methods can be utilized with some success. Such exceptions are few in number compared to others that are easily and effectively examined with the ESDA, even documents written years earlier.[6]

OBLIQUE LIGHT AND
OTHER TRADITIONAL EXAMINATIONS

As already noted decipherment of impressed writing can be accomplished by the same methods as deciphering erasures containing impressed traces of the original matter. The writing impressions are intensified by low angle illumination that creates shadows in the writing grooves, thus making them somewhat more visible (Fig. 8.2). This condition is of help in visual examinations and with photography as well. All the photographic refinements discussed in Chapter 5 involving impressions of the erased material can be adopted to problem at hand.

With extended passages of impressed writing the RCMP oblique light unit produces high quality results as the negative obtained can have a very uniform intensity throughout. Further, uniformly illuminated negatives eliminate uneven prints, common with side lighting from a single light source.

When dealing with writing impressions rather than erased writing, side light examinations can use a lower angle of incident than may be desirable in some erasure cases. The fact that the surface of the paper generally has not been scuffed or disturbed, as it frequently is with pencil erasures, means that indentations are surrounded by a relatively smooth paper surface.

Still there are some problems in which decipherment of the writing is very difficult. Shaneyfelt has found a bas-relief print may be of help.[7] Two oblique light photographs are made, one with light from the right, the second from the left. They are superimposed slightly off register to produce the bas-relief print.

If the page containing the indented writing also has visible writing on it, this overwriting often interferes with the interpretation of the indentations. There are photographic techniques that may either eliminate or weaken the visible writing. Two somewhat common classes of overwriting may be encountered. The first is ink writing that is transparent to infrared radiation.[8] Some colored pencil writing reacts in this way. In such a case the photograph is made with side lighting, an infrared film and a filter that will weaken or eliminate the overwriting while intensifying the impressions (see Fig. 5.8A). The second problem involves colored pencils or inks that absorb infrared, but still can be weakened by photographing with a filter of comparable color to the writing. Such a problem might involve red pencil, which when photographed through a deep red filter is significantly weakened. There are many instances in which either technique only weakens the overwriting, but the indented writing can still be deciphered with greater ease. The reader will find instances in which the overwriting embosses the paper as well so that both sets of impressions are intensified by the photographic techniques. However, the two sets can often be distinguished by the differences in appearance of the colored overwriting and the pure indentations of the impressed writing.

Many of these problems are handled more effectively with the ESDA, which may show a limited sensitivity to the impression of the overwriting or may record overwriting in some instances as white on grey background rather than the black of the impressed writing.

Gayet suggests a technique of photographic superimposition that can be utilized as a means of eliminating or weakening the overwriting.[9] Two negatives of identical enlargement are made: the first under normal illumination; the second, with oblique lighting. A positive transparency of the first negative is prepared on a thin-based film, such as Kodalith Ortho type 3. This positive transparency is exactly superimposed on the second negative and a print made. The resulting print should contain the indented writing with the overwriting eliminated or greatly weakened.

Iodine fuming may help to intensify the writing impressions. The iodine deposits tend to accumulate more in the grooves than in the surrounding area. It has been this writer's experience that with indentations from pencil writing this procedure does not produce very satisfactory results. However, with impressions of typewriting of typebar machines with fine line typefaces and fabric ribbons results were better. Such machines produce strong, sharp impressions, more intense than current impact printers with plastic printwheels and fonts with wider strokes. The deeper, sharper impressions, and possibly the invisible ribbon solvents of the earlier typing, seems to collect iodine deposits more readily. In most instances visual or photographic methods are the more effective techniques.

Another alternative is the use of a fluorescent powder. If the sheet is dusted with a fluorescent powder, finely ground granules will accumulate more readily in the writing grooves. Prior to selection of the powder, it is advisable to examine the paper under ultraviolet radiation to determine its fluorescent qualities and to select a powder that will contrast well when exposed to the ultraviolet radiation. Some writers advocate the use of black fingerprint powder for dusting indentations. This procedure has serious disadvantages when it becomes necessary to remove the powder after dusting. Complete removal is extremely difficult. The remaining fragments of the black carbon can become wedged in the paper fibers and thus suggest that the indentations were the result of a pencil erasure rather than the pure writing indentations. With fluorescent powders, which do not contrast with the paper fibers under normal lighting, fragments remaining after the main portion of the powder has been removed do not cause comparable confusion.

This writer has used the term dusting for the application of these powders. It can be accomplished with a soft brush like one would dust an object for fingerprints. Alternatively, powders can be deposited along the edge of a sheet and by tapping or tilting the sheet cause them to spread in a thin layer across the surface. I. W. Evett suggests dusting a partially inflated balloon and rolling it gently back and forth across the area in question.[10]

D. Graham and H. C. Gray have utilized 200 mesh lead powder to dust the area of indentations, removing the excess lead by means of a rubber roller moistened with acetone and then using hard X-rays to photograph the radiation from the lead dust in the grooves.[11] There is no indication that this technique has been used by other workers.

A. C. Wells has demonstrated the use of radioactive sulphur dioxide as a means of deciphering writing indentations.[12] He describes the method as follows. "The enhanced SO_2 uptake can be made visible by autoradiography after bringing the paper specimen into contact with radioactive $^{35}SO_2$ (1ppm SO_2 at a specific activity of 100mCi/mMole) in a chamber at a relative humidity of approximately 50 percent for a period of 30 minutes. If X-ray film (Kodirex KD-54T is suitable) is placed in close contact with the paper specimen subsequent to the $^{35}SO_2$ treatment, the soft beta radiation (167KeV) from the ^{35}S associated with the paper will automatically expose the X-ray film, giving a positive image of the latent writing. This autoradiograph would require an exposure of about 12 hours." His experimental test show good image reproduction.

There are some other useful methods discussed in earlier chapters. Ronchi plates or "optical contrasters," described in Chapter 4, are a possible tool for reading and photographing impressed writing. With overwriting present a plastic replica of the impression helps to eliminate the interfering writing and to provide a reproduction of the impressed writing. The method of replica preparation is found in Chapter 7. Finally, a word of warning about the technique of intensify the visibility of indentations by rubbing the surrounding paper surface with the side of a soft pencil. It may outline the impressions clearly, but the method has serious shortcomings. Results are not uniformly successful. Furthermore, removal of the pencil lead is difficult, and the same interference is present as was discussed when the document is dusted with black fingerprint powder.

WRITING INDENTATIONS AND ERASURES

Writing indentations on a page of a notebook or bound document may assist in determining what had been erased or altered on the previous page. The indentations found on the page may be from the erased and substituted writing. However, if the pages in question were attached to the altered page after completion, such as the case when several individual sheets are stapled together to form a single document, the impressions may only be the new material inserted after the erasing. This establishes a time before which the change could not have been made, but will not assist in deciphering the original writing. In either case the impressed writing can play a significant role, depending upon the circumstances of the case.

In a problem involving the collision of two ships a series of entries in one of the ship's logs were inconsistent with the collision damage. It was believed that the log must have been altered after the accident, but no evidence of an erasure could be found. When the following page was examined two sets of intermingled indentations were found (Fig. 8.4). One could be related directly to the existing entries on the questioned page while the other had no counterpart to any other writing in the book. Both sets were typical of maneuvering entries. Had a page been torn out? The logbook was loosely stitched with unnumbered pages. Each page was part of a double page sheet, one half in the front portion of the log, the other in the back half. By tracing the two pages under investigation to the other half of the sheets it was clear that the continuity of entries was interrupted. Here was clear proof that the intervening sheet of two pages was missing. This evidence, plus decipherment of the indentations, was proof that the entries concerning the collision had been rewritten.

CONCLUSIONS

Some problems involving decipherment of indented writing relate to erasures and alterations in a document. Others may reveal information about documents in the hands of another party, such as a memorandum written on another sheet of a tablet. Regardless of what value the recovered information may have, the methods discussed will reveal something of the text of the impressed writing.

Notes

1. Osborn, Paul A.: Indentations and anonymous letters. *J. Forensic Sciences, 9,* 1964, 265.
2. See ESDA Chapter 5 for background data.
3. Ellen, D. M., Morantz, D. J. & Foster, D. J.: The use of electrostatic imaging in the detection of indented impressions. *Forensic Science International, 15,* 1980, 53.
4. Noblett, Michael G. & James, Elizabeth L.: Optimim conditions of examination of documents using an electrostatic detection apparatus (ESDA) device to visualize indented writing. *J. Forensic Sciences, 28,* 1989, 697.
5. Giles, Audrey: A controlled humidity environment for ESDA (Unpublished).

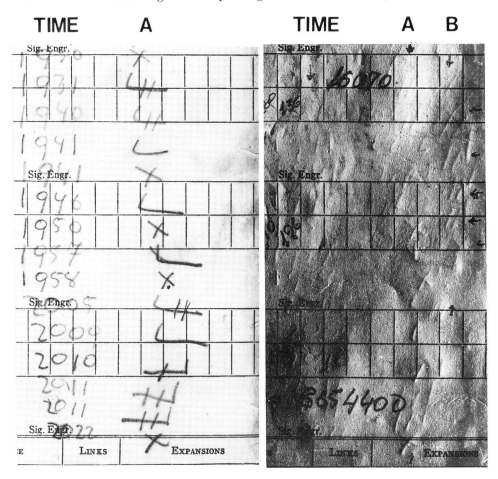

Figure 8.4. Key entries in a ship's log were believed to have been altered (left section). There was no evidence of any erasing. Examination of the page behind them contained both impressed traces of these entries (right, column A) and a second set of comparable entries (column B). No corresponding original entries of the second set were found in the book. These latter impressions formed confirming evidence that a page had been removed from the log and revised.

Read at the 1987 meeting of the American Society of Questioned Document Examiners, Aurora, Colorado.

6. Horan, G. J. & Horan, J. J.: How long after writing can an ESDA image be developed? *Forensic Science International, 39,* 1988, 119.

7. Shaneyfelt, Lyndal L.: Obliterations, alterations and related document problems. *J Forensic Sciences, 16,* 1971, 331.

8. Hilton, Ordway: Traced forgeries and infrared photography. *International Criminal Police Review,* #159, June–July 1962, 195.

9. Gayet, Jean: A method of superimposed photography applied to criminalistics. *J Criminal Law, Criminology and Police Science, 44,* 1953, 379.

10. Evett, I. W.: The decipherment of impressions in paper — some methods old and new, *J Forensic Science Society, 13,* 1971, 83.
11. Graham, D. & Gray, H. C.: The use of X-ray electronography and autoelectronography in forensic investigation. *J Forensic Sciences, 11,* 1966, 124.
12. Wells, A. G.: A novel method for revealing unintended handwriting impressions on underlying layers of paper. *J Forensic Science Society, 16,* 1979, 201

Chapter 9

DOES THE DOCUMENT CONTAIN ERASURES?

At this point it is well to stop to consider the problem of examining the whole document for evidence of erasures. What is the best method of procedure? What things should be done, and in what order should the various techniques discussed in the preceding chapters be most effectively applied? When an erasure is found should decipherment be undertaken before a further search is made for other erasures?

Obviously, the first step is to establish definitely whether there has been an erasure. In so doing it is not necessary to direct all one's attention exclusively to this determination. If an erasure is located, or if there are traces that suggest this condition, the preliminary investigative steps may extend to at least a partial decipherment before one is certain that something has been erased. We should recall that similar techniques are used to carry out both steps. Once it is clear, however, that pencil writing has been removed from the paper, the emphasis naturally turns toward ascertaining what was originally written. This second step may be postponed, however, until the balance of the document has been searched for additional erasures, especially related ones. Changes in dates, amounts, or other details may require other related changes in the document. Whether there are such changes can have a bearing on deciphering the original erasure and its significance.

A review of the third, fourth, and fifth chapters gives the student worker a full insight into the steps necessary to determine whether there was an erasure. Certainly, the areas in which there may have been an erasure should be first defined and delimited by visual study. Disturbed or discolored paper surface, residue of former writings or indentations, singly or in combination, suggest erasing. Before visual study has proceded far some kind of side or oblique lighting will be utilized, possibly combined with photography for confirmation and making a permanent record. If the steps fail to reveal an erasure, it may be desirable to turn to the various special physical and chemical techniques discussed in chapters six and seven to locate a very skillfully executed erasure.

The chief advantage of starting with a visual study is that the examiner determines early what methods should give the greatest promise of successful decipherment. He will know a good deal about any erasure found by the evidence that establishes its existence. Except for the most obvious erasures the examination will have moved well into the phase of decipherment by the time all the evidence of erasing has been evaluated. Certainly, one should have begun to select the better decipherment techniques for the problem at hand.

In a search for erasures one may have to start without any indication whatsoever as to what part of the document may have been tampered with. A careful and orderly examination of the front and back of the sheet is required to localize suspicious areas. On the other hand, those who are interested in the document may have very definite ideas about the erased area and its location. At times these ideas seem highly intuitive to the scientific examiner, but more often they are dictated by the analysis of its contents in the light of the individual's ideas or knowledge of how it was originally written. Other elements relating to the document, as for example, an entry of a particular time or date, may suggest that this portion of the document alone could have been altered. The document may contain other alterations, but the particular entry or entries questioned are the only ones pertinent to the matter under investigation. In such instances the expert's work is definitely limited, but unless it is clear that other changes have no bearing on the problem at hand, the examiner should definitely search the entire document for alterations as well as the section designated by the interested parties. Other changes, when revealed, sometimes become very significant and indicate more extensive fraudulent acts than were suspected initially by those close to the case.

Once the erased area has been located, all steps are normally directed toward deciphering what was removed. Problems of pencil erasures vary greatly. The amount of material removed and subjected to attempted decipherment may range from a single numeral or letter to several paragraphs. In certain problems symbols peculiar to a particular kind of record keeping are erased and changed. Symbols used aboard ship for speed changes or chemical formulae are examples. Similar types of shorthand are used in other records. The change of a single character or symbol can be highly significant. With longer entries, the erasure of one or two words and substitution of some others can change the meaning of an entire sentence.

The intensity of work on individual strokes depends on whether a single symbol or letter was removed or whether several words or a whole sentence were eradicated. With a single character, it becomes essential to reconstruct a significant portion of it from the fragments in order that the character can be accurately deciphered. With several erased words, clear decipherment of a few letters and partial decipherment of material between may lead to an accurate determination of the meaning of the words that were taken out. Thus, in approaching the reconstruction problem one important step is to ascertain the extent of the erasure. With this knowledge, one knows whether initial concentration must be directed toward small elements or toward key fragments with the hope they will suggest decipherment of more extensive passages.

The writer favors starting the actual decipherment process with visual and photographic techniques as set forth in chapters four and five. Just how these techniques are applied is dictated by the problem.

Visual study under daylight conditions is a natural starting point. If it reveals writing fragments in the form of partial erased writing, intensification by photography should follow. It can be acheived with a carefully processed negative that preserves the maximum detail with some increased in contrast or by using either a high contrast film or infrared sensitive material. More than one of these negatives may be prepared so that slightly different photographs are available for study in particularly difficult problems. Writing indentations suggest further visual examination under carefully controlled oblique lighting of varying intensity, supplemented by oblique light photography with both low intensity illumination and some type of spotlights. There will be some problems when the next step will be to utilize the special aids discussed in Chapters 6 and 7. Combination of partially erased graphite and indentations should lead to combining several visual and photographic methods.

When dealing with an extensive erasure one or more well-made photographs are particularly useful in conjunction with further visual examinations. The photographs should be made early in the examination. The combination of photographic and visual study of the original document permits marking of writing fragments on the photograph—fragments that can be recognized either in the photograph or on the original document. In this way one can gradually put together large portions of the erased matter. The reconstructed fragments in turn may suggest a more complete wording of the original text.

When studying photographs it is always well to refer back to the original document to verify, if possible, interpretations of decipherments or actual apparent erased material. For example, indentations revealed in a photograph of writing impressions from another sheet may appear to be very similar to those of erased writing but are more readily distinguised with further study of the original document. Study of the original in conjunction with the photograph is needed to disclose evidence of erasing or fragments of the original pencil graphite. Without evidence of this nature one must conclude that the indentations came from some other source and do not represent erased pencil writing. By the same token, flaws in the paper or unusual fibers recorded in a photograph can suggest writing fragments. Microscopic and visual study of the original document, however, will establish the true source of these apparent writing fragments.

Previous experience with erasure problems normally suggests the pattern of procedure. In some instances early in the examination the various physical and chemical techniques, as well as those marginal or auxiliary procedures for photography and visual study, may seem appropriate because of the conditions encountered in a particular erasure problem. Some chemical methods are most effective before the document had been handled extensively. They usually should be applied early, if at all, but if very careful handling is restricted to a minimum, that is, refraining from touching the suspected area with one's fingers or other objects, some other tests may be carried out first. One must decide, however, before applying any test, whether the particular technique is going to interfere with the application of others that might be utilized later. It is for this reason particularly that the writer normally undertakes visual and photographic studies initially, attempting to decipher as much as possible before turning to other techniques. These two standard methods not only allow subsequent application of other methods, but what is more important, normally give the highest probability of success.

When the suspected erasure is on a page of a bound book there are some special approaches to an attempted decipherment. The area of the following page under the erasure should be carefully studied for traces of indented writing. They may be both indentations from the writing over the erased area intertwined with those from the original writing. This condition can exist in cases in which the erased area is badly disturbed by the erasing action so that indentations from the original writing are confused by the disturbed paper fiber, but the following page does not have these interfering disturbances. With all erasures the back of the erased sheet may contain impressions from the original writing as well as the new material when the writing had been done with the paper on a pliable surface. With writing in a bound book the following pages provide such a surface and the back of the erased sheet may reveal traces of the indentations of both the original and substituted writing.

THE UNERASED DOCUMENT[1]

With any problem in which there has been an erasure of pencil writing this fact may be disclosed by a single examination or by a combination of two or three tests. If, on the other hand, the document has not been erased, this fact cannot be established positively by any single test. The fact that there has been no erasure can only be verified after studying the document in virtually every manner that might reveal an erasure. Each test must give a negative result, i.e. no evidence of erasing. Only then can one say with at least a reasonable degree of certainty that no writing has been removed.

To establish that the document is without erasures requires searching for any evidence that an erasure has occurred following the steps set forth in Chapter 3. Visual study under various lighting conditions with and without magnification, possibly supplemented by other special tests are needed to answer questions such as: Are there disturbed fibers? Writing impressions? Fragments of graphite? Discolored areas of the paper or differences in its reflective qualities? Thin spots in the paper? Each of these occurances may be associated with an erasure. If all fail to appear, we have evidence pointing toward a conclusion that the document is free from erasures.

In the course of answering these questions one must establish that there are no writing fragments that cannot be related to the writing of the document as it now reads. If there are fragments, can they be explained by chance contact of a pencil with the paper? If an area of the paper displays evidence of stains, are they typical of erasure stains or from foreign matter resulting from careless handling or poor storage conditions.

Writing indentations can be found in a document that are not the result of erasing original writing. If such indentations are present, they must be studied thoroughly and carefully. Indentations from previous writing should align properly with the adjoining text. If they have resulted from an erasure, they are very apt to contain small or microscopic fragments of pencil graphite. With some erasures the pressure grooves are clean, but the surrounding area displays other evidence of erasing, a change in the reflective quality of the paper surface, disturbed fibers, slight stain from the rubber or other evidence of its application. If the original writing pressure was heavy enough to create pressure grooves, the complete removal of the previous writing requires extensive rubbing that is very apt to create such evidence. At times the erasing will remove graphite from the original writing, but some small fragments may be caught along the edge of a paper fiber adjacent to the remaining writing groove. Are any fragments present? In evaluating the meaning of suspected indentations, their alignment relative of the other writing may suggest that they are the result of writing on another paper while it rested on this sheet. These observations stress the importance of thorough analysis of this class of evidence in establishing accurately its source and significance.

In some instances smears of pencil graphite fragments are found on a document suggesting that there has been an erasure. These fragments, however, may actually be offsets from other pencil writing, especially writing prepared with a very soft lead and containing intense strokes. They can be distinguished and recognized by careful study. Since the fragments may not be complete words or letters, they suggest that something has been erased, but there is no other evidence consistent with this conclusion. Furthermore, if the fragments are extensive enough to suggest the outline of a letter or part of a word, the form is found to be a mirror image of letters rather than actual writing fragments. The decision between erased fragments and offsets rests upon critical observations.

In many cases the most critical erasures are those that were made after the completion of the text. This can mean that the revised writing must be fit into a limited space with the result that the words or letter may have to be condensed and crowded or in other situations spread out more than the balance of the writing. In searching for an erasure in a document either condition can call attention to where one might have occurred. In establishing that there was not an erasure any suggestion of crowding needs to be given special attention. It is always possible that a change in a document can be made by simply inserting something in a convenient blank space with the same appearance as rewriting after an erasure, and the crowded appearance results without an erasure. If the wording is critical to the meaning of the document the problem may require other examinations despite the conclusion that there has been no erasure. If, on the other hand, no crowding of writing is found, this too is helpful in reaching an opinion that there has been no erasure.

In searching for possible erasures one may come upon writing that suggests a change of pencil. This condition calls for detailed study of the section containing such evidence. The most thorough study must be made before concluding that there has not been a very thorough erasure of some original material. If an erasure is disclosed, the change of writing instrument suggests that the alteration was not made during the preparation of the document, but more likely at a later time. If no erasure is found, then the question may be raised whether this material was inserted in blank area of the document and was not part of it originally. This problem may be difficult to answer, but analysis of methods of solving it is beyond the scope of this monograph.

Pencil-written documents with clearly undisturbed areas around all the writing present no serious problems. After applying all tests for detecting possible erasures, especially for very skillful ones, one can state with strong confidence that nothing has been effaced. The difficult problems involve those that have been pointed out in which some smudges or indentations appear. In these instances one cannot conclude casually that an erasure had occurred. It is always necessary to evaluate all apparent indications of erased writing to ascertain whether something has been removed. Pencil erasures normally contain more than a single criterion of erasing. When such combinations are present, it is very clear that there was an erasure. On the other hand, only a lack of a combination of factors pointing toward an erasure, together with a logical counterexplanation for any suspicious physical condition that may be present, allows one to conclude that the document is free of erasures.

Notes

1. This section is derived from the author's earlier and more extensive article: Proof of an unaltered document. *J. Criminal Law, Criminology & Police Science, 49,* 1959, 601. The material had been translated into German by Dr. Albert Kraut and was published: Der Beweis fur die Echtheit eines Schriftstucks. *Kriminalistik, 12,* 1958, 459. Also refer to: Hilton, Ordway: *Scientific Examination of Questioned Documents,* 1982, New York, Elsevier, 122.

Chapter 10

DATING ERASURES[1]

At this point in the text the reader must appreciate that the problem of establishing what was erased is challenging. A further question, "Can you tell when the erasure was made?" substantially increases the challenge. The examiner normally considers this one unanswerable. He knows that the chances of revealing the absolute date are remote and should undoubtedly be considered virtually impossible. But to establish when the erasure was made in relationship to the preparation of surrounding writings or to subsequent handling of the document may be accomplished under favorable circumstances. Even so, failures will well out number successes. Limited determinations of this nature may still be significant in a particular problem, and with many erasures some thought ought to be given to when they were made.

Erasing while a document is being written carries different implications from erasing after completion. Most fraudulent changes fall in the latter group. Study of the physical conditions in the immediate area of the erasure, on the back of the sheet, or on the next sheet below the erased area serve as a way of distinguishing between these two classes of changes. This assertion presumes that some definite or suggestive dating evidence is present, which of course is far from true in every case.

It takes great skill to remove writing thoroughly without disturbing adjacent writing in any way. Greater skill and dexterity is needed when the words and lines are closely spaced than with wider spacing. Still with relatively wide spacing there are generally certain instances when lower and upper projections of letters approach very closely or actually impinge on the writing of the adjacent lines. The complete erasure involves removal of the lower loops or projections of "y's" and "g's" or the upper projections of "h's", "l's" and other tall letters as well as their middle sections.

Fortunately, most people in making an alteration are more intent on removing the writing than on avoiding the adjacent material. Thus, any damage to writing in an area that was not changed must be carefully analyzed. This can be an important clue to when the change was made. Some damage to the following lines in particular is a clear indication that these lines were on the paper when the erasure was made. On the other hand, if the paper surface under these lines shows any evidence of the rubbing action, and if there is no damage at all to the writing in this area, the change certainly was made before the line was executed (Fig. 10.1).

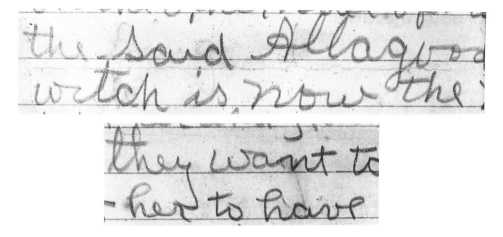

Figure 10.1. In a pencil-written holographic will the testatrix made several obvious erasures as she composed the will. All were partial erasures with graphite smears or writing fragments and were completed before the next word or line was written. In the upper section "said" appears over the erasure of "Alag" the first part of Allagood and then all of Allagood was written. Several lines below, "way" was written, the "y" erased and the word completed as "want." The lower projection of the erased letter falls in the area of "have" on the following line which is undisturbed showing that the erasing was completed before "have" was written. In both cases the characteristics of the erasures and the surrounding writing establishes the order of erasing and writing.

In approaching dating questions consideration should be given to folds, creases, perforations, and the like in the erased area. What is the order in which the erasure and these other acts took place? There may be no way of independently establishing when the folds, creases, or perforations occurred, but the sequence of the strokes of both altered and unaltered writing across such a disturbance may have significance. Furthermore, the sequence of intersecting strokes as determined from the writing in the erased area and the next line, when these do intersect, may shed light on the relative time of erasing. The sequence determinations in the case of pencil writing are difficult at best, and often no clear-cut decision can be made, but the problem should certainly be investigated.

By the same token, the spacing of the writing over the erased area and the adjacent unerased lines can assist in answering the question of when the erasure occurred. No doubt crowding or spreading of the writing over the erasure compared to the other lines can be convincing evidence that the change followed the completion of all of the original writing; while consistent spacing throughout the page suggests, but may not prove conclusively, that the change was made during preparation.

As emphasized in the preceding paragraphs, the makeup of the document has a direct control on any estimate of when the erasure occurred. It is also true of documents that were originally written on separate sheets of paper before being assembled into a multiple page unit. When an erasure occurs on a page of such a document a careful study should be made of both the following sheets and the back of the sheet in question. If the altered words alone are embossed on the next page but none of the original writing, one concludes the change came after the original preparation and assembly. If some offset fragments from the following sheet are found on the back of the erased area we have further evidence leading to the same conclusion. In contrast, if the back of the altered sheet shows embossing throughout and none carried through to the next page, the change probably occurred during original preparation. In some instances, however, the physical evidence does not clearly decide the issue especially with light writing pressure that fails to create any embossings.

A case example illustrates the importance of dating information in litigation. A pencil-written desk diary contained dated entries. Some of these were being used to substantiate testimony of a witness. One key entry had been extensively rewritten by the simple process of erasing words and putting in new matter. The change occurred at points within all three lines and included a change in the last line of writing. The next item, which was started on the following line, was dated several days later (Fig. 10.2).

Studying the writing immediately above the erasure disclosed that when words on the last line were taken out, the erasing process had weakened some of the pencil strokes in the line above. Furthermore, fragments of the original erased writing appeared throughout the lines and some lower loop letters on the last line had projected closer to the next line of writing than the tall letters had to the line above. The

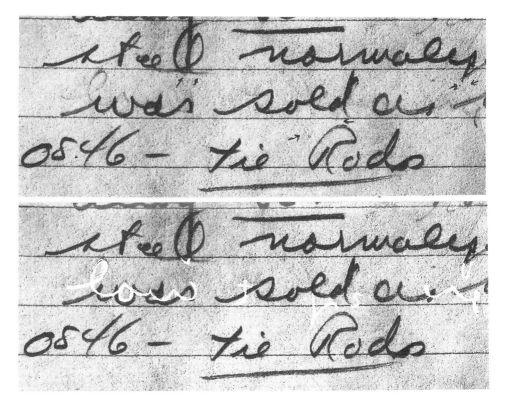

Figure 10.2. Arrows point to slight damage in the lower tip of a "y" from the line above "steel" and the ending of its final "l" when "low" on the next line was erased. Continuing along the altered line further damage to writing of the first line occurs in the lower portion of the "z" of "normalized." In contrast no damage occurred to the "R" of "Rods" when the "p" of "temps" (best interpretation of the erased word) was removed. The "0846" entry was dated several days after the altered entry. Physical evidence is consistent with the change in the altered entry having been made before the "0846" notation was written.

subsequent entry had suffered no damage from the erasing in contrast to the conditions found in the line above. Analysis of the evidence tends to establish that the entry had been corrected at the time of writing or within a short timespan before the next item was written three days later. A change after the following entry had been made was ruled out. If the change occurred just after the entry was first made, the witness was probably telling the truth; but if it had been several years later when this case was being prepared for trial or just before he was to testify, his testimony had no weight. While what had been erased could be significant, when it was done was far more important.

In the problem at hand both bits of information had similar significance.

What had been erased compared to the rewritten memorandum did not constitute a substantial change in meaning. When it was possible to show the strong likelihood that the changes had been made soon after the memorandum was first written, within three days, the total expert evidence took on added weight.

The full investigation of any erasure includes consideration of when it was made. Just because it may be more common for it to be impossible to establish any significant dating information, this condition should not preclude consideration of the problem in every case. It would be just as illogical to say that since there are instances in which the erased writing cannot be completely deciphered one should stop every examination as soon as the examiner discovers that there was an erasure and never attempt to find out what was erased. We are responsible, in the interest of justice, to seek out all the facts and indications that are buried in the document. There will be an occasional case in which the relative time of the erasure may far out weigh the significance of what was erased.

Notes

1. This chapter is based on a section of a paper presented at the 1966 International Meeting in Questioned Documents, Copenhagen. The full text, translated into German by W. Hofmann, was published as, Entzifferung ausradierter Schriften, *Kriminalistik, 22,* 1968 385–388. The English version was republished with permission of Kriminalistik as: Special considerations in deciphering erased writing, *Journal of Police Science and Administration, 13,* 1985 93–98.

Chapter 11

ASSOCIATED EVIDENCE[1]

The chief aim in deciphering erasures is to discover what has been removed. Decipherment normally is tedious and time-consuming, but under some conditions the ultimate answer can be ascertained quickly and accurately by other means. Carbon copies of the altered paper, duplicate originals, a series of interrelated documents of which the erased one is an integral unit or a forgotten photocopy made as a routine step before the erasure may contain the information that normally is only derived through deciphering the erased matter. This associated evidence may disclose convincing proof of what has been erased. With it and a demonstration of the erasure on the questioned document itself, there is little room for argument about the ultimate solution despite the most fragmentary decipherment.

The term "associated evidence" embraces all documents that in anyway are related to the pertinent contents of the altered one and may thus assist in its reconstruction. It may be a carbon copy, a smooth draft made from altered rough pencil notes, other entries related to the altered one in a record or log book, all documents that are prepared in connection with a transaction, such as a purchase or sale, or an index or entries on file cards referring to a completely erased item. Knowledge of how the erased document fits in a business record system may tell where to look for the duplicate or related entries.

Present-day business practices use many pencil written documents as part of their record system or office procedure. When an erasure is under investigation, it is important to have knowledge of the whole procedure. It is surprising how often an erasure is made on a single document, even by someone familiar with the associated records, without modifying the accompanying records (Fig. 11.1). Those interested in reconstructing the erasure, however, are also prone to forget about the associated documents. If the alteration was made subsequent to the original preparation, the associated documents may not be available to the culprit, and he must depend on his altered document being accepted at face value. Unfortunately, for those who suffer from the change there are a certain number of instances that this occurs.

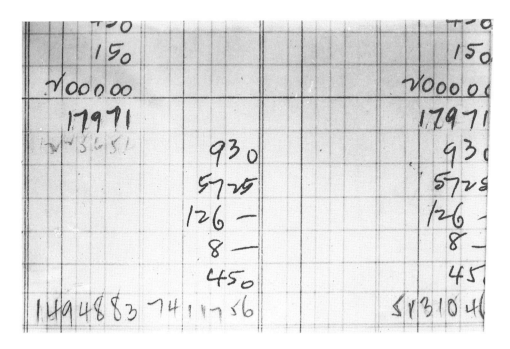

Figure 11.1. Associated evidence, a bank deposit slip, verified the decipherment of erased and altered figures in a ledger. The left-hand column lists bank deposits. The dark ink entry, 179.71, is the only line written with ink of this color on the page. The right-hand column, accounts receivable, has a corresponding black ink entry. There is evidence of erased inks in both columns, which can be deciphered as 704.71. The fragments of erased ink was similar to the unaltered entries on the page. Penciled subtotals were also changed. 14948.83 was originally 15473.83 (the 4 doubtful) and 51310.46 was 51835.46. Each erased entry was greater by 525.00, an amount that appeared in the dark ink on the following page. The bank deposit slip listed all checks in corresponding order on the two pages except checks for 179.71 and 525.00. Instead one check of 704.71 appeared after the 2000.00 check.

At the start of every erasure problem a careful inquiry should be made into how the suspected document was prepared and how it was used. When this information is fully developed, it may become obvious, for example, that there is a carbon copy that has not been located. When found, it frequently is completely unaltered, especially if the erasure is a fraudulent one. On the other hand, if the copy is also altered, the erasing may not be as thorough. In such cases should only fragments of both erasures be deciphered, they may be correlated to achieve a more extensive, complete decipherment than is possible from either of them individually.

Both copies may have been changed to correct an error at the time of preparation or, on the other hand, may have been erased to commit fraud. Sometimes the custody of the two copies may decide this issue while in other instances knowledge of what was erased helps in reaching a decision. In the latter situation the more completely the erased matter can be deciphered the better chance there is that the tryer of facts or others concerned with the problem will be able to reach an accurate decision. In any event, location of all papers that in any way relate to the erased one or its preparation may play a part in determining what was erased as well as evaluating the significance of the act.

A brief example or two emphasizes the value of associated evidence.

A tailor's record book that consisted of numbered stubs was produced to establish an alibi that the suspect was in a city some distance from the crime scene. The stub in evidence contained clear indications of an erasure. The book was carefully indexed. With the stub number a search was made of the index and a second name was found in addition to the one written over the erasure. The second name simplified decipherment of the erased writing and confirmed its accuracy besides virtually destroying the value of this alibi evidence.

It is usual practice aboard ship to keep a duplicate record of changes of speed, one in the deck or bridge log and one in the engine room log. In admiralty cases involving ship collisions, critical maneuvers and changes of speed immediately before the accident are closely scrutinized. These books are traditionally kept in pencil. There are instances in which key entries have been erased and rewritten. Whenever there is a suspicion of a self-serving change in a deck log, the engine room log should also be studied. Many times if one has been fraudulently altered, both are found to have been erased. Not only is there a better chance to establish what the original entry was, but also the opposition's assertion that the change was merely a correction in one log at the time that the entry was made may be overcome.

Associated evidence is sometimes created by chance. If the erased document was part of a tablet, a notebook, or a group of bound, detachable sheets, writing impressions are often transferred to the following sheet during the preparation of the questioned material. Decipherment of these writing impressions may be an effective way to reconstruct what has been written before an erasure or to supplement decipherment of the erased sheet. It also may indicate when the erasure was made, as we saw in the previous chapter, depending upon when two sheets were bound together and whether the altered wording is impressed on the next sheet. With two pages that were either separated or assembled after original preparation indentations of this kind may also disclose that some matter was added in a convenient blank space in a document after preparation even though no erasure had been made. These writing indentations in documents of the kind under consideration substitute for the carbon copies upon proper laboratory development and have the further advantage that the writer himself is unaware of their existence.

Modern offices tend to utilize photocopy machines more and more. Some offices photocopy originals in lieu of carbon copies since they can be prepared easily and quickly. One should always ask whether the erased paper may have been copied and if so, how were the copies distributed or filed. Careful investigation or inquiries may locate a copy of the document before the change. Then complete decipherment of the erasure may no longer be essential.

This discussion must not be concluded without pointing out that an erasure can be reconstructed from records that are not exact copies or duplicates of the original. Accounting records, inventories, or statistical data often are based on a series of working records. If the altered data in the erased document should have been developed or compiled from several source documents, working from the unaltered source units can assist in reconstructing and verifying the decipherment of the erasure. All material in any way related to the questioned document can assist in confirming the work of the document examiner.

The significance of associated evidence rests in the fact that the investigation of a suspected document does not necessarily end with its technical examination. There often exists these other related documents that contain very forceful evidence on how the suspected document must have read originally. Furthermore, when fraud has been attempted these supplementary papers may destroy any attempt to explain away the erasure as merely a correction made while writing the document.

Notes

1. This chapter appeared as a portion of an article published in *Kriminalistik*, 1968 and is used with their permission. See note 1, chapter 10.

Chapter 12

WHY INCOMPLETE DECIPHERMENTS

Attempts to decipher erased pencil writing are not always successful. There are cases in which the most that can be said is that there has been an erasure. In other instances some decipherment of the original writing is possible, but not all. Several factors may limit the findings. The erasure itself may have been very thorough and may have gouged and disturbed the paper surface extensively (Fig. 12.1). The presence of overwriting in the erased area can seriously interfere, while creases and folds around the erasure restrict some useful decipherment techniques. The writing may be difficult to read even when all the letters can be seen. Serious mishandling of the document before submitting it to the document laboratory can destroy some of the details that assist in a decipherment. With an erasure of foreign language writing, the examiner's lack of fluency or thorough understanding of the language may limit his findings. Then there are cases in which the nature of the effaced writing itself may present further difficulties, especially when prepared with a very light pencil stroke. Looking over this list of restrictive elements may make one wonder how so many erasures are deciphered successfully.

CONDITION OF THE ERASED AREA

The actual erasing process sometimes limits decipherment. Seldom is it necessary to wear a hole or a very thin spot in the paper to remove all the writing, but poor quality papers or a highly abrasive eraser may cause such a condition. There are erasures encountered from time to time in which the paper surface is badly disturbed and even discolored. With these conditions the extent of decipherment normally is limited. Actually there may be the occasional case in which the person erasing is very persistent and thorough and with moderately weak original writing practically no traces will be left on which to build a decipherment. Unless some writing ridges remain on the back of the sheet, there is very little the examiner can do to bring about a decipherment.

Figure 12.1. The order number 9888 was written over an obvious erasure. The area shows fragments of a former number, badly disturbed paper surface and some smearing of pencil graphite. Decipherment of the original digits was impossible, except for the left fragment that suggests a "9." Heavy overwriting, thorough erasing of the other digits and lack of any writing embossing combine to prevent a successful decipherment.

OVERWRITING AND FOLDS

Writing over the erased area may obscure or interfere with study of the erased strokes. Depending upon what is written, and how it done, some or almost all of the original writing is obscured. A heavy pencil and a broad stroke have a tendency to partially or completely cover the original writing fragments (Fig. 12.2). Under such circumstances it may not have been necessary to remove much of the original writing. The overwriting may effectively mask and obscure most of the remaining strokes.

In earlier chapters we have seen the importance of examinations under critical lighting conditions, especially oblique lighting. If the paper surface cannot be completely flattened, it becomes very difficult to study slight writing indentations. It is seldom that a crease or fold falls exactly over an erased stroke, but it may create interfering shadows and prevent the most effective lighting of the suspected area. When the erasure consists of only a few letters, a deep crease near it is a severe handicap. Not only is it apt to restrict decipherment, but it may cause false interpretations that must be carefully checked or hide some of the weaker writing indentations. Thus it should be a strict practice *not to introduce new folds.* Keep handling to a minimum. Place the document in a clear plastic folder so that both front and back can be examined and read when needed. Such cover should prevent wrinkling and the introduction of accidental creases.

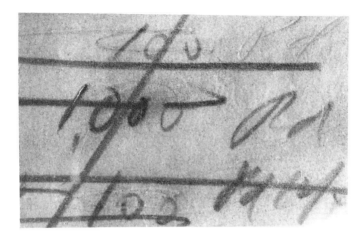

Figure 12.2. Heavy writing of the first three digits "100" hides any weak fragments of the original writing. The final "0" was part of the original number and is written with a relatively weaker pencil stroke. Thus erasing is nearly complete. These factors made a decipherment impossible.

Many individuals' handwriting can be difficult to read until one has become very familiar with it. If such semilegible writing has been erased, fully deciphered strokes may convey only limited meaning. When a person habitually writes open "a's" and "o's," u-shaped "m's" and "n's," and fails to dot "i's," and uses many closed "e's," whole words can be made up of a series of u-shaped forms. Except for context, they have little meaning. Thus, a completely deciphered erased word written in this way may at best permit only an estimate of what was originally intended.

When one becomes familiar with a person's writing of this type, the forms tend to take on more meaning. They can also be better interpreted when the erased word, phrase, or sentence is placed in context with other unerased writing. In deciphering effaced writing we have seen that entire words are sometimes suggested by key fragments, and whole sentences, by significant words and word fragments. These deductions must, of course, be very carefully studied and weighed with all other fragments. Partially deciphered erased matter, may sometimes be interpreted in several ways, but once it is clear which interpretation leads to a significant thought or word all others can be discarded provided the remaining fragments also appear to be consistent. In much the same way a person familiar with the semilegible writing of a friend or associate, upon seeing a partial decipherment of erased matter may be able to read much more meaning into the decipherment than as examiner who has no or very limited knowledge of the writer's habits.

To assist in decipherment of difficult writing, as well as in many other erasure cases, it is helpful to be able to study known specimens of the individual's writing, especially his general handwriting. But in spite of all of these aids, there are still cases in which decipherment remains incomplete simply because no one can read or interpret the strokes that can be seen.

AN UNFAMILIAR LANGUAGE

Material in a foreign language is more difficult to decipher than writing in the examiner's native tongue. Progress is slow in deciphering these erasures and results are often limited. The examiner cannot always apply meaning to a sentence or word as a whole and fragments of writing do not necessarily suggest familiar letter combinations as they might in his own language. Unassisted most examiners find foreign language erasures an obstacle to decipherment.

In a measure this handicap can be overcome by conference between the examiner and a person who is fluent in the language. With the examiner pointing out the decipherable fragments and their possible interpretations, frequently the other conferee can supply meaning. At least the extent of decipherment is extended to some degree. In one case involving an erasure in a Swedish ship's log, the keeper of the log was available for consultation. He suggested several possible words for the erased one, but none fit the key parts of the decipherment. Finally, after pointing out several of these letters, the man supplied the missing word and wrote it on a tablet. With this sample the particular word could be verified by comparison of both the prominent and less prominent fragments of the erasure. (Figure 12.3).

NATURE OF ORIGINAL WRITING AND OF THE ERASURE

If the original writing was executed with an unusually light stroke that deposited very little graphite and did not emboss the paper, it is possible to remove almost, if not all, of the original writing. At best an erased light pencil stroke is extremely difficult to decipher. Virtually no carbon remains, and in addition the weak pressure leaves no suggestion of the original writing track. Demonstration of the erasure itself sometimes is

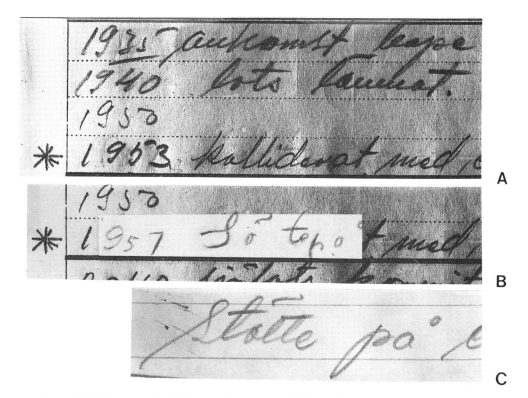

Figure 12.3. The time of collision was first written 1957 and then changed to 1953. This erasure is rather easily read (section A), but the fragments under "kollides at" could not be fully deciphered. Extensive erasing and the lack of fluency with Swedish were the chief factors. When the ship's captain was interviewed, it was suggested that the first word began with "S" and included a "t" after several blanks. He then wrote "Stotte pa" (reproduced in section C). He translated both words "collided with." The decipherable fragments, traced over the obliteration of the overwriting, is shown in section B. A second translator suggested the original words might better be read "ran into," which was consistent with the position of the two ships.

extremely difficult, and decipherment of what had been originally written almost impossible.

Erased writing prepared with a very soft, somewhat dull pencil at times defies decipherment. The erasing process may have discolored the paper so badly that the erasure is obvious, but the widespread smearing of the heavy graphite smudges throughout the suspected area coupled with the lack of either significant pressure grooves or of a fragmentary outline of the original writing prevents interpretation of what was originally written.

CONCLUSIONS

Some of the more likely roadblocks to complete decipherments have been touched upon. The fragments of erased pencil writing furthermore are rather fragile so the excessive handling may also restrict findings. While many problems are satisfactorily solved, we must not expect universal success. Every experienced worker recognizes that there are some cases in which results are at best fragmentary and an occasional one in which almost nothing can be deciphered.

Chapter 13

HANDLING DOCUMENTS SUSPECTED
OF CONTAINING ERASURES

In a measure every document is fragile and excessive handling or mishandling can destroy evidence. Pencil-written documents are somewhat more fragile than others, those with erasures even more so. Careless or even excessive handling reduces the chances of successful decipherment of the original writing. There have been cases in which decipherment has become impossible because of mishandling.

Once a suspected document is discovered every precaution should be taken to preserve it in the condition that it was first discovered. Advice on care of documents has appeared in many questioned document texts and should be familiar to document examiners and experienced investigators.[1] This discussion is primarily designed for those who have had no previous experience in handling documents and especially those containing erasures.

The previous chapter contained some indications of limitations that may occur due to too much handling. Simple advice would be to place the document in a protective folder, clear plastic types are the best. This type of envelope or folder can be obtained at most office supply stores. With a single page in question opened out flat it can be read or examined without subjecting the critical areas to damage or wear. When unprotected, someone pointing at a key area with his finger may leave slight smudges or with a pencil, graphite dots. More important, submit the protected document to the examiner promptly.

All steps in handling a document that may have been erased should be taken to prevent the addition not only of new folds but of minor creases as well. Clipping several sheets together with paper clips can introduce small ridges. Pins and staples should definitely be avoided. They add holes as well as creases. Marking the suspected area is probably the worst thing that can be done. If a person feels the need of such a marking, photocopy the document first on a copier in which the document rests on a flat bed. Then mark the photocopy. Send both to the examiner. This step will not interfere with technical examinations or introduce some questionable marks that could restrict such studies.

When dealing with assembled or bound documents, inner sheets that might be in question are fairly well protected in the course of handling. If pages are unnumbered a long strip of paper can be inserted at the proper page or pages. Here is where paper clips are particularly tempting, but refrain from using them. In diaries or log books, in which the pages cannot be removed, the whole book will have to be submitted. These books should be protected by normal care and packaging. If the bound document is made up of sheets stapled together, it is best to leave them stapled, designating the page by number or by an inserted strip of paper. If the examiner finds a need for separating he can do this, but the following pages may contain writing impressions that are of value to the examiner either in interpreting the erased material or revealing evidence of when the change might have taken place.

A final warning. Do not let any nonexpert or person with very limited experience try to decipher the erasure or to test it in any way. Such a person may be lucky and find an answer for you. If he does not, his lack of knowledge of decipherment techniques may damage a document so that a qualified person cannot proceed with the proper testings. If fingerprints are to be developed wait until the nondestructive decipherment techniques have been made. Ninhydrin testing can damage writing impressions. Properly advised document examiners can study the document without adding new prints or injuring those that may be in the paper. After proper photographing to record any erased writing found, the document can be subjected to chemical development of the fingerprints.

Common sense and care are the most important steps in handling an erased document. Nothing should be done to it that might lessen the chances of deciphering what was erased. Anyone who has carefully studied and understood the methods in this text should have a very good idea of the proper way of handling these fragile pieces of evidence.

Notes

1. See Osborn, Albert S.: *Questioned Documents,* 2nd ed., 1929, Albany, Boyd Printing, pp. 20–24. Also Hilton, Ordway: *Scientific Examination of Questioned Documents,* rev. ed., 1982, New York, Elsevier, pp. 349–360.

Chapter 14

PRESENTING EVIDENCE OF ERASURES—
IN REPORTS AND IN COURT

In the earlier chapters we have been completely concerned with detecting and deciphering erased pencil writing. These steps are important, but it is also important to transmit this information to interested parties in a clear and effective manner. The routine reporting of findings can involve special procedures that are unnecessary in other types of document examination reports. The ultimate step though is the courtroom demonstration to a judge or jury. This phase can only be effective with extensive and careful pretrial preparation by both expert and attorney. The expert's task is to design the clearest demonstration exhibits, which disclose subtle alterations to the inexperienced lay observer. The attorney must understand the importance of these illustrations and make sure that proper pretrial steps are taken so that the expert's exhibit and testimony will not be excluded.

REPORTS

Reports concerning decipherment of erased pencil writing may be one or two types: (1) a simple summary of findings or (2) a report that includes a demonstration of findings. With the first type, it is unnecessary to attempt any illustration of the decipherment. No special photographs are needed; the report simply sets forth the information as to whether there has been an erasure, and if so, what was erased. Except for possible internal use in certain law enforcement agencies such a report is not recommended.

The second type involves a more extensive presentation. Photographic illustrations are included to allow the reader to evaluate the indicated findings himself. Frequently, these photographs reveal the decipherments and their relationship to the balance of the document more clearly than is possible to describe in words. These photographs are similar to ones used for courtroom presentation. In report photographs there may be somewhat greater freedom in marking than with photographs used in court. Examiners should take advantage of this freedom whenever expedient, making sure that the photographs are clearly made a part of the report. If at trial the cross examiner asks for the expert's report for the purpose of cross examination, it can often be put in evidence, and the photographs would be admitted as well. Well marked photographs accompanying the report show the trial attorney their effectiveness and thus convinces someone who has not had experience with this kind of case the need for using these interpretive photographs in the courtroom.

COURTROOM PRESENTATIONS

Testimony concerning the decipherment of erasures takes on added dimensions when accompanied by good demonstration photographs. Even partially-erased writing can be very difficult to read. If the erasure is not extensive enough to cause some difficulty in reading the original writing, it is very unlikely that an expert witness would be required in the courtroom. More commonly, erasures are hard to decipher under the most favorable laboratory conditions. Consequently, testimony can only infrequently be accompanied by a visual demonstration from the document itself. If it is to be anything more than a verbal report by the expert to the court, it must be supplemented by the very best possible photographic decipherments as court exhibits.

Erased pencil writing, as we have seen, requires extensive study. The various fragments that are put together to affect a decipherment must be carefully interpreted. The apparent solution must be tested by review and rechecking. Every examiner who has worked with these problems knows that an individual who inspects the paper with preconceived ideas may see in the fragments interpretations that are not necessarily correct. Photographic exhibits allow detailed discussion and analysis by the witness. With them he can answer intelligently the questions of the court and the cross-examiner, and all can see the physical evidence concerned. In turn, the photographs are available to those who must decide the issue, to be weighed against the examiner's opinion. These significant reasons are why one would not want to present this type of evidence to a judge or jury depending solely on optical aids and special lights to view the original document. Such steps might be used to supplement good photographic demonstrations, but never to replace it.

PRESENTATION PHOTOGRAPHS

Presentation photographs for either reports or courtroom testimony are based on the best possible photographic decipherments that can be made. They should contain the clearest details. Such a decipherment probably should be reproduced at a slight enlargement. Some enlargement is desirable so that the person examining it may do so without any optical aids other than his reading glasses where required. In speaking of a slight enlargement this size photograph is intended to be held by the viewer and not one that would be placed on an easel in front of a jury.

In order to show the decipherment clearly a very effective technique is to mark the photograph with the examiner's interpretation of the decipherment. Even for reports this writer make a practice of hinging two prints together. One copy is unmarked, the other carefully marked with red or other contrasting colored ink. The outline and fragments of the erased writing that appear in the photograph are accurately traced. With the markings in a bright contrasting ink it is easy for the reader of the report, or a judge and jury members, to understand how the witness interprets the writing fragments. The unmarked photograph allows the observer to evaluate critically the accuracy of the interpretation. He can study for himself the original unmarked photograph to decide whether he agrees. This marking technique significantly reduces the verbal statements of testimony needed to explain the photographic exhibit, but with the combined marked and unmarked chart the findings are presented fairly and effectively.

A good working enlargement for these photographs generally ranges between $1\frac{1}{2}$ and 2 diameters. Most examiners agree that in presenting these problems in court such a range of magnification is effective, and individual photographic illustrations should be prepared for each juror or each pair of jurors.[1] This writer prefers a single illustration for two jurors. The enlargement is not so great that the writing fragments become scattered and difficult for the eye to draw together. Still there is enough enlargement that the viewer can see details that might otherwise be unnoticed.

The writer has once attempted to present erased pencil writing using a single very large illustration hung before the jury. The "billboard" type enlargement generally does not produce a very good illustration, but when the negative reveals the decipherment clearly, it can be used effectively. There are opportunities with this kind of illustration to point out exactly the fragments that make up the decipherment and even to mark these points in the jury's presence. It is well even so to supplement such a display exhibit with hand-size copies so that the jurors can critically examine the erasure and the interpretations as they hear the testimony. We must remember that jurors' vision is not tested before they are sworn, and there is always the chance that a particular juror may not see well, especially across a courtroom.

The Witness's Claims Concerning an Erasure

In a manual of this kind, full consideration of the trial of a case involving erased documents is not appropriate. However, the significance of erasures many times depends on the claims of those who are concerned with the document. What the witness says about the erasure may be completely consistent with the facts or totally at variance with them.

Once a pencil erasure has been discovered the party who wrote the document or the altered portion, and anyone who might have had access to the paper and could benefit from the change, should be carefully interrogated. The statements obviously should be taken under oath so that they are binding on the witness. They should be obtained before the examiner's findings are known to the witness. It is generally preferable to take these statements in a pretrial examination or deposition. If this is not done, the witness certainly should be examined during the trial before the examiner testifies. Pretrial knowledge of what interested witnesses may say about the document and the erased portion in particular may determine how significant testimony concerning the decipherment may be. It prevents a witness adjusting his story to fit the facts. Furthermore, if the changes in the document are found to be critical more extensive preparation on this aspect of the case presentation is obviously warranted.

Experienced trial attorneys know how witnesses who are not thoroughly examined on a critical point may be able to explain away evidence adverse to their claims. There have been some cases in which an opposing witness learned before trial about the successful decipherment of a fraudulently altered document. While not everyone has produced a logical excuse for the alteration, each has tried. In all probability if he had been properly examined prior to learning of this fact he would have testified in such a way that any later attempt to explain away the change would have strongly suggested perjury.

We know that many pencil-written documents are erased during preparation to revise or correct them. Presence of an erasure thus does not necessarily prove fraud. Positive statements by a witness, however, can change a very innocent looking erasure into a substantial piece of adverse evidence. In other words, should a person maintain that no change has been made, the erasure may become very damaging, even though it might seem to have had a simple explanation. In contrast, a very obvious and clear-cut change when admitted to and explained without prompting may well have to be treated as described by the witness's statement.

SUMMARY

The presentation of erased writing problems in the courtroom is a challenging procedure. It requires good team work by the trial attorney and expert witness. The writer has discussed in earlier publications the details that should be covered by trial counsel and his expert, both before coming to court and in the courtroom.[2] In a technical manual of this kind they need not be repeated. The steps apply to any type of document case including erasure problems. When an erasure can be successfully deciphered, those who must decide the case are entitled to understand what was erased and to be able to see for themselves what was originally there. Well designed court exhibits and carefully planned testimony can achieve this end.

Notes

1. One of the most definitive studies on presenting photographic charts to jurors is reported by Swett, George C.: The use of individual photographic charts in presenting questioned document testimony. *J Criminal Law, Criminology & Police Science, 42,* 1952, 826.
2. See particularly Hilton, Ordway: *Scientific Examination of Questioned Documents,* rev. ed., 1982, New York, Elsevier, Part V, The document problem goes to court, p. 391, in which both pretrial preparation and courtroom testimony are discussed.

Chapter 15

ADDENDUM—RELATED DOCUMENT PROBLEMS

This addendum surveys problems which have some relationship to erased pencil writing. Many methods of examination previously considered may have certain application. One group of common questions arising out of pencil-written documents involves a suspicion of alteration by addition without erasing. Other problems concern possible erasures of all nonpencil-written documents in which deciphering techniques might be similar to those discussed in this text. It seems inappropriate to deal with these subjects exhaustively in this text, and therefore the presentations will merely outline useful laboratory methods and call attention to the interrelationship between these problems and pencil erasures.

ALTERATIONS IN PENCIL-WRITTEN DOCUMENTS

It is not always necessary to erase part of a document in order to change its meaning. Often the manner in which it was prepared presents an opportunity to insert a word or more extensive matter to make the change. This condition exists with all types of documents, including pencil-written ones. The parties affected may suspect that the document has been erased and rewritten when actually all that was done was to insert a modifying word, a figure, or possibly a sentence, paragraph, or page.

Factors which must be considered with these problems include the following:

1. Is there more than one person's handwriting?
2. Have different pencils been used?
3. Does the pencil condition show a continuous gradual dulling typical of use, or are there sudden changes in sharpness or other writing qualities to raise suspicion of writing at different times?
4. Is there consistent embossing or lack of embossing throughout the document?

5. Are there undue crowdings or unusual margins, especially in the suspected portions of the document?
6. Was a carbon copy, or a photocopy, made and is it an exact copy of the original?
7. Where pencil strokes intersect can the order or sequence be determined? Is it normal or abnormal? Is it consistent with what the witnesses have already said about the way the paper was prepared?
8. If the paper is folded or creased, does the order of writing in respect to the folds remain consistent throughout?

When there has been no erasure, the answer to these seven questions are of significance. Added material may be readily disclosed by unexplained, improper sequence of intersecting strokes, key words written with a different pencil or with a change in the condition of its point, with sharply different pressure traces, or with unnatural crowding. But if all of these factors are consistent with normal preparation of the document or if the physical factors and the witness's statement agree, then suspicions are not founded on fact. Usually, one of the strongest evidences of an insertion is physical evidence that two intersecting strokes were written in an unnatural order or in a sequence inconsistent with the normal or logical manner in which the document should have been prepared.

The problem of determining the sequence or writing order of pencil strokes is far from simple. The writing groove patterns and the striations within strokes themselves arc the most useful key in establishing which line is continuous and which was interrupted. Sometimes all these criteria combine to establish clearly the order of writing, but this is not always true. When pencil strokes and folds intersect, the condition of the pencil stroke where it crosses the fold tells a good deal about the order of writing. With a deep, worn concave fold graphite in the breaks of the paper and skipping across small deep crevices point toward writing after folding while a gap in the pencil stroke where the paper is broken can be evidence of writing before the fold. A convex fold damaged by the pencil's action at the point of intersection must have been made before the writing. Further microscopic skipping of the pencil on the far side of the fold after the pencil crossed the raised portion establishes the same sequence. Some pencil strokes written before a convex fold may show a slight break at the top of the fold.

Microscopic study of the strokes under carefully controlled lighting, in which both the angle of viewing and of illumination can be varied, produces the most satisfactory results. Accurate determination of the sequence of pencil strokes, however, is not easy. A number of special techniques have been suggested, some more useful than others. Unfortunately, many pencil intersections fail to reveal any clear-cut evidence of sequence due to such common limiting factors as light writing pressure, excess handling, and the type of pencil used, among others. Certainly, it is inappropriate to consider the problem more in detail here, and a reader with a specific problem should refer to other sources for procedural details.[1,2]

When there is a probability or suspicion that a whole page might have been added or substituted, the first six factors detailed at the beginning of this section are pertinent. There is also need to consider the paper itself — whether the suspected sheet is or is not consistent with the others. Watermark, dimensions, color or tint, and other physical qualities must be carefully investigated. How the pages are bound together and whether there is evidence or suggestion of rebinding becomes important. So does any other physical evidence that might prove or disprove the unity of the present pages.

With a multiple page, bound document made up of sheets normally assembled after writing was completed, addition to one of the pages may be disclosed by study of the following pages as well. Writing indentations of parts, but not all, of the contents of the page before suggests writing at two separate times with different backing condition. The embossed and indented strokes must have been written after the sheets were assembled, especially if indentations on the following page are in proper register with the writing of the page before. Even if the entire page in question shows embossing and only a few suspected words or sentences are impressed on the next page, there is clear evidence of the insertion after assembly.[3]

Many of the visual and photographic methods used to detect and decipher erasures can be used in these problems. The ESDA and oblique light photography play a significant role in alteration by insertions. The need to establish that there has been no erasure is often the first step in these problems.[4] The reader will also find other methods of help in a particular instance.

Certain of these factors are encountered in a document with an erasure. But erasing would not be necessary if the document had originally been prepared with gaps in which the insertions could be made between the lines or sections. Documents can be modified either by erasure or by simple additions. The alert examiner must be prepared to find and disclose evidence of either method of alteration.

Obliterations

Obliteration of pencil and other writings is accomplished by covering the original writing with heavy pencil strokes or ink and other material to hide the original entry. Pencil is very often completely or partially obliterated by a series of pencil strokes sufficient to obscure all of the writing, or at least enough of it, so that it cannot be read. In these cases it is extremely difficult to decipher what was originally written. The overwriting cannot be erased since the original pencil writing will also be removed. If there are suggestions that the original writing embossed the paper and the strikeout did not, or may have left weaker embossings, it may be possible to attack the problem by an oblique light photograph of the back of the sheet. Or in the same way an infrared photograph may show a more intense outline of the original writing than the covering strokes. If some portions of the pencil writing shows between the obliterating strokes, an enlarged photograph of it is helpful in studying these fragments. At best with good luck and perseverance a partial decipherment might be achieved.

Decipherment of ink and typewriting obliterated by covering with pencil, ink, or white-out requires consideration of the characteristics of the original writing material and the covering substance. At times the cover can be erased manually, as with pencil over ink, or removed with solvents, as with ink or white-out over pencil or typewriting. However, the usual first steps are visual or photographic techniques. The underwriting may be deciphered by infrared, infrared luminescence, or oblique light photography to penetrate the cover.[5] Attack from the back of the sheet with these types of photographs or even transmitted light should be tried. To repeat again, whatever degree of success is gained requires trial and experimentation.

OTHER ERASURE PROBLEMS

Erased Typewriting

Altered or erased typewriting may have been prepared originally by the older typebar machines, manual or electric; or the single element electric and electronic typewriters, both the typeball (IBM Selectric® and others) and print wheel printers which are part of electronic typewriters, word processing units, or computer printers. The more common electronic printers that produce work comparable to earlier electric typewriters are of the impact type, in which the letters are printed by typefaces striking against an inked ribbon. The vast majority of these ribbons were and still are black. Originally, they were inked cloth ribbons, but for some years now they have had a film base. The most common ink is a permanent black carbon ink. However, with the introduction of the lift off device on machines, a new type of ink was needed. The black ink is compounded so that it can be completely lifted off the paper by restriking the letter through a lift-off tape. The permanent type impression will be considered in the following paragraphs leaving lift-off ribbon impressions for later discussion.

In the typing of a document the raised letter outlines strike the ribbon causing some ink to be pressed on the paper surface. The force of the blow drives ink into the crevices of the paper fiber and causes some ink to adhere to the fiber surface as well. All permanent inks are very difficult to erase, requiring an abrasive eraser to remove the ink, thus roughing the paper surface appreciably.

The condition of the document after typewriting has been erased is similar to its condition after a pencil erasure. There usually are slight indentations of the original typewriting. There is also apt to be at least some deposit of the original typewriting ink. Paper fibers, however, are normally more disturbed than with pencil erasures; thin spots in the paper, more common. Frequently, there are stained areas on the back of the sheet beneath the erasure. Decipherment depends on intensifying and studying the remaining carbon and interpreting the impressed outlines. It is clear that in deciphering erased typewriting one can certainly start with techniques applicable to pencil erasures. The most effective include visual examination or photography with side lighting to read the embossing and photographic intensification techniques, including high contrast and possibly infrared photography, to emphasize and to study the remaining inks fragments. The ESDA may assist, but it appears less useful in typewriter problems than other writing impressions. The reader, however, will do well to consider all methods for deciphering erased pencil writing since normally there are very few which do not have some application to typewriting problems.

One advantage in deciphering erased typewriting is its uniform spacing. One only has to study the unerased portions of the document to know exactly how much space each letter occupies. Furthermore, letter design is repeated with greater uniformity than with handwriting. With an appropriate test plate one can locate accurately where the erasures took place and determine the maximum number of letters which could have originally occupied the space. When only fragments of characters are deciphered, they can be related to the machine's type design and its more obvious defects. In this way it is often possible to establish the presence of certain letters very convincingly without reconstructing their entire outline. Consider, for example, the curving lower projection of a "y" as compared to the lower projections of a "g" or other extensions below the line, or the position of the vertical staff of a "d" in relation to the vertical staff of an "h" or other tall letters. Knowledge of the type face designs and the accurate positioning of erased letters are excellent starting points for deciphering any typewriting.

Overtyping in the erased area very likely will not be in absolute alignment with the original typewriting, though it still makes decipherment more difficult. In such a case the back of the page can be studied for traces of the embossed impression of the original typewriting. Erasing typewriting is difficult; decipherment of the original matter may be arduous and time-consuming.

The introduction of the lift-off process simplified the attack on finding and deciphering alterations. When typing a document, it is possible to erase letters or words easily. Simply backspace to the point of correction or change, place the machine in the lift off mode and retype the letters or words to the left of the typing position. Then type the correction or change over the erased space. With a machine in good operating condition the lifted letters will remain only as a clear indentation of the erased material. They can be read by an oblique light photograph or simply under oblique lighting if the impressions are clear. Remaining ink is neglible to nonexistant.

If the copy has been removed from the machine it is still possible to lift the typing off the paper with tacky lifting material. However, after several days it is much more difficult to accomplish a clean lift off of the typing. Still the ink is erased more readily than permanent typewriting. Often it can be accomplished when fresh with a soft pencil erasure. If adhering more firmly, then erasing becomes much the same as with permanent typewriting ink. It is extremely difficult to reinsert the paper in the typewriter to use the lift-off device. Attempts generally lead to double clear impressions almost overlapping and some remaining ink around the erasure.

Carbon Copies

In the most modernized businesses carbon copies are rarely used. File copies may be computer disks or tapes or photocopies of the original document. But for many years carbon copies, even two or more, were made simultaneously with the original document. The document examiner today can still encounter altered carbon copies, especially erased ones.

The extensive erasure of carbon copies, either handwritten or typewritten, are achieved by mechanical erasing, particularly using a rubber eraser. Extensive erasing necessary to remove virtually all of the carbon deposit may require a course eraser and can created a very rough or discolored surface, clearly revealing the site of the erasure. Normally, writing fragments that remain form the cornerstone to the decipherment.

With black copies the marking material is primarily carbon; with colored "carbon sheets," dyes or lakes. Carbon copies tend to be devoid of indentation from either the writing instrument or the typewriter, although a search should be made for the rare grooves before abandoning decipherment techniques based on embossing. The ESDA is well known for its ability to read pressure patterns that cannot be seen visually and should be tried on all altered carbon copies. The marking substance is deposited on the paper surface or forced into the fiber crevices, but does not penetrate the fibers themselves. In general the examiner concentrates on those methods which involve the intensification of fragmentary outlines and carbon deposits. Photographic methods used to decipher erased pencil writing can be needed to effect the most extensive decipherments.

When dealing with an erased carbon copy, never forget to search for the original copy or another carbon copy. It may be found unerased and unaltered. If so, you have your decipherment.

Contemporary Pens

Present-day pens are made up of several distinctively different types. The oldest of the group is the ballpoint pen, which is probably the most widely used. In addition there are the fiber or soft-tip pens, the porous or plastic tip pen, and the roller pen.[6] The ballpoint pen uses a paste like ink; the others all use some type of fluid ink, a modification of the earlier bottle inks that were used with the dip, steel pen and the fountain pen. Because of the composition of the inks used in the pens of today, each presents its own problems involving erasures.

The standard ballpoint pen in one form or another has been in use since the 1940s.[7] Except for the erasable ballpoint pen, which will be discussed in a later paragraph, ball pen writing is very difficult to erase. The paste like ink is rolled on the paper under pressure penetrating in the crevices between the paper fiber and staining and bonding to the fibers themselves. It is not easily bleached by fluid eradicators. Erasing is usually accomplished by rubbing with a gritty eraser, such as a typewriter eraser. With perseverance this instrument will remove the ink but at the same time damage the paper fibers leaving a rough, disturbed area. Normally, weak fragments of ink remain. If the paper is not too badly damaged, some of the writing grooves, which are a typical characteristic of the ball pen writing, may remain. The back of the sheet often reveals these pressure patterns more clearly. Techniques of deciphering pencil erasures, such as oblique lighting and contrast photography, are useful. Occasionally, the ESDA may be of assistance, especially if the text had been written on a pad and the sheets below can be located.

The erasable ball pen uses a special ink which, when fresh, is easily erased with a pencil eraser.[8,9] Some fragments of ink may remain in the erased area, but the original writing grooves of the ball are not apt to be damaged. Decipherment techniques are obvious for intensifying these writing grooves.

Soft or fiber tip pens deposit a heavy ink line even with finer points. The ink penetrates the paper fibers and is not easily removed. Remaining fragments can be intensified photographically, and if the ink absorbs infrared radiation, infrared and contrast photography may be helpful. Ultraviolet and infrared luminescence, which are not too helpful with pencil erasures, can sometimes assist in revealing the partially erased ink lines.[10]

The same observations are true with erasures of writing of a porous, plastic point pen. These pens when used to write on a soft surface, such as a tablet sheet, may create a slight indentation of the writing line. If the erasing is not so extensive that the paper surface is seriously damaged, these writing grooves may be intensified with oblique light photography. ESDA examination of the pages below the writing may also develop the original text.

While the roller pen's inks stain the paper fibers the ball itself makes the characteristic groove pattern of a ballpoint pen. So examination methods previously discussed with ball pen and pencil writing grooves are applicable, and infrared, ultraviolet, and infrared luminescence techniques should all be tried.

CONCLUSIONS

The problems touched on in this chapter warrant more extensive considerations. However, it was not the intent of this monograph to expand on the methods needed in these problems. If a worker becomes familiar with the methods for handling pencil erasures, he has at hand methods that can be applied to other kinds of problems. The brief discussion is an introduction to solving each of these kinds of erasure problems as well as other pencil writing problems.

Notes

1. Godown, Linton: Sequence of writing. *J. Criminal Law, Criminology & Police Science, 54,* 1963, 101–109.
2. Bradley, J. H.: Sequence of pencil strokes, *J. Criminal Law Criminology & Police Science, 54,* 1963, 232–234.
3. Greer, K. E.: Unusual photographic techniques in document examination. *Forencis Science, 7,* 1976, 23–30.
4. Hilton, Ordway: Proof of an unaltered document. *J. Criminal Law, Criminology & Police Science, 49,* 1959, 601–604.
5. Shaneyfelt, Lyndal L.: Obliterations, alterations and related document problems. *J Forensic Sciences, 16,* 1971, 331–342.
6. Hilton, Ordway: Distinctive qualities of today's pens. *J Forensic Science Society, 24,* 1984, 157–164.
7. Stein, Elbridge & Hilton, Ordway: Ball point pens: Questions raised by examiners of signatures and documents, *American Bar Association J., 34,* 1948, 373–376.
8. Flynn, William J.: Paper Mate's new erasable ink pen, *J Police Science and Administration, 7,* 1979, 346–369.

 9. Hilton, Ordway: Characteristics of erasable ball point pens. *Forensic Science International, 26,* 1984, 269–75.
10. Chowdhry, R., Gupta, S. K. and Bami, H. L.: Detection and decipherment of erasures in documents, *J Forensic Science Society, 16,* 1976, 139–150.

INDEX

Shading with pencil, 68
    warning against, 68
    writing impressions, 68
Silicone rubber, 69
Smudges
    no erasure, 15–16
    sign of erasure, 12
    (*also see* Graphite)
Sulphur
    detecting erasures, 19
    radio active sulphur, writing impressions, 77
Superimposed negatives, 55, 76

T

Thin spots
    detected by dye solution, 20
    erasure evidence, 12, 14, 86, 115
    typewriting erasure, 115
Transmitted light
    combined with oblique light, 59
    use in erasure, 14, 28
Typewriting erasures, 115–116
    evidence of, 115
    lift-off ribbon changes, 116
    pencil erasure methods useful, 115
    problems with overwriting, 116
    test plates and uniform spacing, 116

U

Ultraviolet radiation
    deciphering erasures, 30
    fluorescent dusting powders, 67, 77
    limited value, 30
Unerased document, 86–88, 113
    evaluation of suspected erasures, 88
    first step with altered documents, 113
    no single test for proof, 86
    offset pencil not erasure fragment, 87

W

Witness's claim re erasure, 109
    need to establish, 109
    influences importance of decipherment, 109
Writing impressions
    (*see* Impressed writing)
Writing stroke
    fragments of, after erasure, 13, 15
    inconsistent with erasure, 16
    sequence across fold, etc., dating aid, 90
    sequence of, in alterations, 112
    suggested erasures, 16
    very light strokes limits decipherment, 98, 101